Jonathan Dodson gives thoughtful counsel on how to communicate the gospel to our secular culture today. He is right on target. He is honest. This is evangelism for the twenty-first century—and for all centuries, for that matter!

—Robert E. Coleman, Distinguished Professor of
Evangelism and Discipleship at Gordon-Conwell Theological
Seminary, and author of *The Master Plan of Evangelism*

How did it happen that the gospel we preach has been rejected as bad news by our culture? In *The Unbelievable Gospel*, Jonathan Dodson opens up this puzzle. Reading it gave me confidence, liberated my imagination, and gave me a pathway to an evangelism that lives the gospel as well as tells it. It is a stunningly clarifying book.

—David Fitch, Lindner Chair of Evangelical Theology,
Northern Seminary, and author of *Prodigal Christianity*

What is unbelievable about *The Unbelievable Gospel* is that its message is so needed and we haven't had a well-written practical book on it until now. Jonathan Dodson really cares about how the church is talking to the world. He has demonstrated as much in his personal life, especially how he continued to hold his own feet to the fire in the first years of his church. He would not accept numeric church growth as success, for he had higher standards. His genuine humility comes through as he tells the church what it needs to hear and how it can talk to the world so they will listen. The contents of this work could educate and set free a congregation to communicate the gospel effectively with the people they care about.

—Bill Hull, author of *The Disciple-Making
Pastor, Christlike, The Disciple-Making Church,*
and *The Complete Book of Discipleship*

D0068571

The gospel does not change, but we must always be attentive to how we can best communicate it afresh to each generation. Jonathan Dodson in *The Unbelievable Gospel* demonstrates, once again, that he is one of the church's leading thinkers in knowing how to present the gospel effectively in an increasingly postmodern world. I highly recommend it!

— Timothy C. Tennent, **President, Asbury Theological Seminary, Professor of World Christianity**

If you are passionate about the gospel but despair at the difficulty of communicating the good news of Jesus in the urban, creative contexts of the West, then *The Unbelievable Gospel* is for you. A compelling and empowering guide to sharing faith today.

— Mark Sayers, **Red Church in Melbourne, Über, and author of** *The Road Trip That Changed the World* **and** *Facing Leviathan*

There is no doubt that we need to rethink much about the way we have shared the gospel in America. So much of our evangelism bears false witness to the very gospel we seek to promote. Jonathan's thoughtful and well-researched book provides both a great antidote and good guidance at the same time. Anyone interested in the integrity of the gospel and how it is communicated should read this book.

— Alan Hirsch, **Founder of Forge Missional Training Network and Future Travelers; award-winning author of numerous books, including** *Untamed* **and** *Right Here Right Now*

There is always a need to communicate the unchanging gospel using language and forms that can be understood by emerging generations. If you have a passion to share the good news of Jesus, this book is for you."

— Darrin Patrick, lead pastor of The Journey; vice president of Acts 29; chaplain to the St. Louis Cardinals; author of *The Dude's Guide to Manhood*.

Over the past decade, I've sifted through boatloads of books related to spreading the message of Christ's gospel. I have poured slowly through the most popular books on the subject, but have always found myself longing for something more. *The Unbelievable Gospel* contains what my heart has been yearning for: an evangelistic manifesto that every Christian should read. It is the best evangelism book I've ever read, by far.

— Matt Brown, evangelist, author of *Awakening: Why the Next Great Move of God Is Right under Our Nose*, founder of Think Eternity

All of us encounter not-yet Christians on a daily basis, and for one reason or another, we often fail to engage these people with the greatest story ever told: the gospel. We each come to the table with reasons for not sharing Jesus. Jonathan brilliantly gives us a soul-check and reminds us that evangelism can be winsome and fun when done with a heart transfixed by the person of Jesus and his work in the world. For those of us without the gift of evangelism, Jonathan encourages us that, yes, we can indeed share a believable gospel — not because of who we are or what we do, but because of what our great Savior has done for us.

— Laurie Fortunak Nichols, editor of the Evangelvision blog, director of communications at the Billy Graham Center at Wheaton College, and managing editor for *Evangelical Missions Quarterly*

This is a wonderful book, one that I will repeatedly return to for my own edification and encouragement and will gladly urge others to read. This is a book for pastors and ministry leaders as well as for all Christians. Jonathan's book will not make you feel guilty and ashamed that you are not a great evangelist, or that you are an inadequate one or a poor one; but this book will encourage and motivate you to think about evangelism in new and helpful ways.

—Jerram Barrs, Francis Schaeffer Institute at Covenant Theological Seminary, author of *Learning Evangelism from Jesus*

I am so glad to see a book that addresses both why we struggle to share a gospel that actually is good news while also giving us helpful and accessible ways to share the truths about Jesus that speak to the heart and needs of real people. Jonathan has given us a tool that will greatly serve the church in this present age we live in; it is not formulaic and rigid, but a book that is both solid and fluid.

—Jeff Vanderstelt, pastor at Soma Communities

People who have yet to meet Christ in a life changing way through the gospel are not stupid—they can tell if we care for them, or if they are simply a project to us. In this fantastic book, Jonathan Dodson incisively slices away at our failed, broken attempts to share Christ—without being hypercritical. He opens our eyes to the beautiful and unbelievable gospel and offers practical, biblical metaphors for sharing Christ today. We can be winsome and intentional in our witness, and Jonathan shows us how. Every believer should read this!

—Alvin L. Reid, professor of evangelism and student ministry/Bailey Smith Chair of Evangelism at Southeastern Baptist Theological Seminary

THE UNBELIEVABLE GOSPEL

GOSPEL

Say Something Worth Believing

Jonathan K. Dodson

 ZONDERVAN®

ZONDERVAN

The Unbelievable Gospel
Copyright © 2014 by Jonathan Dodson

This title is also available as a Zondervan ebook. Visit www.zondervan.com/ebooks.

This title is also available in a Zondervan audio edition. Visit www.zondervan.fm.

Requests for information should be addressed to:

Zondervan, 3900 *Sparks Dr. SE, Grand Rapids, Michigan 49546*

Library of Congress Cataloging-in-Publication Data

Dodson, Jonathan K.
    The unbelievable gospel : say something worth believing / Jonathan K.
Dodson.
        pages cm
    ISBN 978-0-310-51669-9
    1. Witness bearing (Christianity) I. Title.
    BV4520.D64 2014
    248'.5--dc23   2014015653

Published in association with Yates & Yates, www.yates2.com.

Cover design: FaceOut Studio
Interior illustration: Brendan Pittman, Electrik
Interior design: Matthew Van Zomeren

Printed in the United States of America

14 15 16 17 18 19 20 21 22 23 24 /DCI/ 20 19 18 17 16 15 14 13 12 11 10 9 8 7 6 5 4 3 2 1

To George Landrum Dodson (Poppa)
Always an evangelist, whether on his knees or in the pulpit

CONTENTS

ACKNOWLEDGMENTS

When I was awakened to the beauty of Christ as a child, I soon began to devour missionary biographies. Some of my childhood heroes include Bruce Olson, Samuel Morris, C. T. Studd, Hudson Taylor, and Amy Carmichael. The Holy Spirit blew through these stories, instilling a love for Christ, the lost, and the mission of God. In particular, I am grateful for my deceased grandmother, "Mother Joyce," who stirred my passion and even introduced me to real, live missionaries! Her husband, "Poppa," not only serves as an example of dedication to the gospel but also prays regularly for me. I get special attention in prayer on Wednesdays. He has prayed me through many things, particularly in planting and establishing City Life Church. Thank you, Poppa.

A number of churches and missions organizations have played an important role in training and sending me to communicate the gospel to neighbors and "the nations." They include Denton Bible Church, Cru, OMF, and Bethlehem Baptist Church. The experiences I gained through these churches and organizations laid a foundation for the rich missiological training I received at Gordon-Conwell Theological Seminary from Tim Tennent, who made a strong academic, missionary, and pietistic impression on me. His teaching helped me see the world and engage its cultures the way I do. His influence undergirds much of my missionary task of preaching, witnessing, and church planting. I admire you, Tim.

Some of the great evangelistic models in my life include: Jerry McCune, Chris Allred, Paul Dreblow, Steve Niphakis, Nate Navarro, Tyrell Grohman, Doug Birdsall, and my grandfather, George Landrum

Dodson. I am grateful for their example of earnest faith and their gracious deposit in me.

My parents' devotion to Christ, extraordinary love, and unceasing prayers carried me through some of my own wandering years. I shudder to think who I would have become were it not for their constant witness and deep, missionary faith. Mom and Dad, "thank you" is not enough.

A special word of gratitude to the team at Zondervan—Ryan Pazdur, Jesse Hillman, and Verlyn Verbrugge. Your editorial suggestions and belief in the book were helpful and a genuine encouragement. To my agent, Sealy Yates, thank you for believing in me and for being more than a literary agent.

Thank you, City Life, for seeding these pages with authentic stories of mission as we work together to renew cities socially, spiritually, and culturally with the gospel of Jesus. I can't imagine doing this with anyone else.

As always, nothing is written without the unflagging support of my delightful companion, co-laborer in the gospel, and remarkable wife, Robie. Thank you for freely giving me time to write and think, and for championing this book by living out its message with me. I love you.

Finally, I acknowledge my infinite debt to God the Father, the Son, and the Holy Spirit, whose grace led me into the gospel that is forever worth believing. I love you *because you first loved me.*

PREFACE

Evangelism has become a byword. It has fallen to the wayside in Christian vocabulary. Some see it sitting in the gutter; others walk by without noticing at all. Some have replaced it with missional; others have replaced it with social justice. Still more are aware it is there but deliberately avoid it, *and with good reason.*

RECOVERING FROM EVANGELISM

Evangelism is something many Christians are trying to recover from. The word stirs up memories of rehearsed presentations, awkward door-to-door witnessing, and forced conversions in revival-like settings. We can now add "fake baptisms" to the list.[1] To be certain, God may use these efforts, but not as much as is often claimed.[2] In fact, these forms of evangelism have actually created an impediment to evangelism. Wave after wave of rationalistic, rehearsed (and at times coerced and confrontational) evangelism has inoculated, if not antagonized, the broader culture. In response, Hollywood has taken up its own evangelistic message in documentaries like *Jesus Camp* and films like *There Will Be Blood, Saved!, Philomena,* and *Believe Me.* The public has been disaffected by our evangelism.

Though it is unintentional, "modern" forms of evangelism have generated gospel witness that is impersonal, preachy, intolerant, and uninformed about the real questions people ask. These encounters result in not much witness to the gospel at all. Such repeated experiences create a distaste for evangelism, not only in the mouths of non-Christians but also among Christians. Many Christians have quieted down in their witness to avoid creating a preachy, impersonal, intolerant, and uninformed impression. They don't want the gospel to be misunderstood.

To be clear, I am not interested in beating up particular evangelistic methods. However, I do think it is important that we pause to reflect on our evangelistic heritage, our current cultural moment, and consider plausible reasons why people today have an aversion to evangelism. To do this, we must recognize that twentieth-century American evangelism worked because the culture was largely familiar with Christianity. It included several assumptions, such as the brute fact of absolute truth, the existence of heaven and hell (or God for that matter), and a widely held notion that sin keeps us from God.

We can no longer assume this understanding. Today, many Christian teachings and assumptions are fuzzy, even questionable to most people. Calling people to "repent and believe in Jesus" is typically misconstrued as "stop doing bad things, start doing good things (like Jesus did), and God will save you." This, of course, has nothing to do with the gospel and leaves us disconnected from our culture. There is a considerable gap between the gospel communicator and the receptor culture.[3] This gap is filled with all sorts of things that prevent effective gospel witness, including theological misunderstandings and unbelievable forms of evangelism. How can we turn down our evangelistic noise and cut through the cultural confusion in order to communicate a clear, winsome gospel message? The challenge of regaining cultural credibility, polarizing evangelism, and personal evangelistic concerns must be addressed. If we are to regain credibility and warm people to evangelism once again, we must respond to these evangelistic defeaters (part 1), recover the nature of the true gospel (part 2), as well as chart a wiser, more patient, and discerning way forward (part 3).

GETTING TO A BELIEVABLE GOSPEL

After witnessing across the globe for thirty years, being trained with all kinds of evangelistic tools, and making disciples in the local church, I continually encounter a fundamental question that is often overlooked:

How is the gospel good news to those we evangelize?

Not *what* is the good news, but *how* is our news good for others? Christians are often proficient at rehearsing the information of the gospel, but we often lack the ability to relate the gospel to the lives of others. For some reason we find it difficult to bridge the gospel into everyday life and everyday unbelief. If we are to overcome our obstacles to evangelism, we must be able to answer this question: "What does the death and resurrection of a first-century Jewish messiah have to do with twenty-first-century people?"

How does the gospel transform the self-righteous do-gooder, the skeptical urbanite, the distant spouse, the successful professional, and the strung-out addict? These people can be us — Christians — and they can be others. If we have trouble getting the good news into these ruinous predicaments for ourselves, how then will we relate the redeeming hope of Jesus to others in similar situations? Please don't mishear me. I'm not saying that the hope of salvation rests on us. It is hopeful to know that, in the end, the Holy Spirit has the final say in convincing others that the gospel is good news. But along the way, the Holy Spirit chooses to use what *we say* to others.

The gospel is good news whether someone perceives it to be good to them or not. But the only reason we know it is good is because we experience its grace-saturated goodness in our everyday lives. We know the gospel is good, not just in theory, but in the experience of suffering, parenting, dating, working, and so on. We know the gospel is good because it frees us from being a slave to others' opinions, when through faith in Christ, we have obtained the opinion that matters most — God the Father saying, "You are my son; with you I am well-pleased!" This deep, undying love and approval of God the Father frees us from people-pleasing, over-working, spouse-impressing, self-adoring living. The gospel sets us free! The trouble, of course, is that there are so many people who don't know the power of the gospel in this way. They don't know *how* the gospel is good news for them.

If Jesus did die and rise for the world, then it is incumbent on us, his followers, to tell others *how* and *why* the gospel is good. Reciting a memorized fact that Jesus died on the cross for sins to a coworker doesn't tell them why it is important or how it can change their life. Reciting this information dispassionately is even less convincing. What people need to know is not only what the gospel is, but what the gospel does. Otherwise, asking people to believe in a tortured, invisible Jewish messiah, for no apparent reason, is *unbelievable*. The problem we face, then, is not simply an issue of what to say but how to say it. We are challenged to share the gospel in a way that is worth believing, both with ourselves and others.

My aim, then, is to recover a *believable* evangelism, one that moves beyond the cultural and personal barriers we have erected in contemporary evangelism to rediscover the power of the biblical gospel. To recover a believable gospel we must do two things. First, we must consider why we tend to avoid evangelism. We will consider four types of unbelievable evangelism that lead many Christians — people who genuinely love Jesus — to avoid sharing their faith. I call these *evangelistic defeaters*. Second, we will take a deeper look at the gospel itself to rediscover the diverse and multifaceted ways God has designed his message of good news to speak to the heartfelt needs and pain of those around us. What makes the gospel *believable*? Third, we will look at five *gospel metaphors* — justification, union with Christ, redemption, adoption, and new creation — to learn how each of these different gospel images can be applied to different people in different circumstances.

In order for our evangelism to be believable, it must be biblical. So when we communicate the gospel of grace, we must necessarily draw on biblical truths, stories, and images. If we stop there, however, we will fail to communicate effectively *how* the gospel is good news to others. Like good counselors, we must listen to others well to know how to effectively communicate the unsearchable riches of Christ in a way that speaks to their unique life story.

My hope is that the Lord will use this book to stoke fresh fires of belief in the gospel for Christians who have forgotten why the gospel is good news. I also eagerly hope and pray it will help us to better communicate the unsearchable riches of Christ to those who are not yet in

Christ. By God's grace, perhaps this modest investment will assist in moving evangelism from a byword to a believable word, one that truly offers grace and hope to a lost and confused world.

chapter one

WHY PEOPLE FIND THE GOSPEL UNBELIEVABLE

I'm not an evangelist. I haven't led thousands to Christ. There won't be a long receiving line of eternal souls waiting to thank me at the golden gates of the New Jerusalem.

This used to bother me. I grew up in an evangelical household in the deep pinewoods of East Texas, where revivals were announced in advance. The church marquee announced the date and the evangelist came to town. The goal was to invite your friends to come hear the preacher. He would preach and people would come to Jesus.

Altar calls have a long history in East Texas, locally known as the "buckle" of the Bible Belt. My grandfather, a godly man and a faithful Baptist preacher, led many down the aisle by calling them to bow a head, slip up a hand, or come to the front to make a decision to follow Jesus. Although I did not personally respond to God's stunning offer in Christ in this way, the call was still clear when I heard the gospel at a young age, and my grandfather was there a few weeks later to baptize me when I went public with my faith.

Wind the clock forward a few decades. After those East Texas revivals of my youth, I had the opportunity to travel the globe telling people about Jesus. But as much as I tried to leave Texas, I found myself drawn back (much to my surprise). Together with my wife, we planted a church in Austin, the countercultural capital of our conservative state. Some call Austin "the hole in the Bible Belt." It has a religious outer rim and a countercultural urban core. It's a "weird" and wired city.[1] Until his recent death, Leslie Cochran, an elderly homeless man with a boob job and a tutu, was the unofficial icon of the city. Austin hosts offices for many tech firms: Dell Computers, AMD, Apple, Google, Dropbox, just to name a few. It's a city that teems with creativity, a counterculture attitude, and remarkable subcultural diversity.[2] Though most of Texas leans to the right, Austin is a "blue dot in a red state."

Austin is where I live. It is the city where I labor to embody and communicate the gospel every day. We moved to Austin to plant the gospel and to plead with God to grow a church. At that time, my wife was pregnant with our second child, Ellie. Today, in addition to our own children, we have been blessed to welcome a new community of spiritual children as well. But critical to that process has been learning how to effectively and appropriately evangelize. After all, we didn't move across the country, from Boston to Austin, just to recycle Christians from other churches. We came to Austin because it's a decidedly non-Christian city, and we want to serve its people and bring them fantastic news about Jesus. That meant we needed to know the city, love the city, and engage the city in meaningful and discerning ways.

I studied anthropology in college, so I knew I had a lot to learn about the diverse subcultures of Austin. We studied. We observed. We conversed. And in our research, we learned that 76 percent of the city's urban core finds the gospel of Jesus *unbelievable*.[3] This was a helpful, humbling, and inspiring discovery. Aware that we were living with resistant, not just "unchurched" people, we knew that evangelism was needed, but in a way far different from the altar calls of my youth.

DEALING WITH FAILURE

During our first year in the city one person — one single individual — came to know Christ. It was a small success, but soon, even that seemed short-lived. Soon after he professed his faith and for the next four years, it looked as if our initial convert had walked away from his new faith. Thankfully, today he is back in church and is thriving in Christ. Still ... one person in a city of 1.7 million? In one year? Not a great start.

I found some comfort in our poor track record by telling myself that we hadn't *really* started our church yet. We were still in that learning phase: transitioning into the city, studying the culture, and hosting a small group of people in our home once a week. So it really wasn't fair to start counting yet. Right? Our small group of people grew into a community, and together we rediscovered the mission of God. We got to know our neighbors and engaged the city in ways that visibly demonstrated the love of Christ and offered the hope of the gospel. The number of non-Christians in our circles steadily increased. Still, after two years of ministry in Austin, we had only baptized one new disciple. We had gone to Austin hoping to reach hundreds, if not thousands of people.

One person. I was discouraged. I felt like I was failing.

As the years passed, we saw a few more people respond. We were now averaging about three to five baptisms a year. And yet, new questions arose in my mind. Were we doing enough? Did our "conversion rate" justify the costs, personal and financial, that we had made in planting the church? Was it worth it to relocate our family and deal with the intense spiritual warfare we were under? Most of all, I wondered: *If I was leading our church correctly, equipping our people well, shouldn't we be seeing more results? Was I doing something wrong?*

I felt a vague evangelistic pressure. Perhaps you can relate. I'm not sure where it comes from, but it entered my atmosphere in my early twenties. Back then, everywhere I went, an evangelistic cloud seemed to follow me. Preoccupied with the eternal destiny of others, I frequently felt compelled to share the gospel, and if I missed an opportunity I had a sense lightning would strike. Guilt traveled down my spine whenever I wimped out and didn't share. Avoiding an opportunity on an airplane was especially unforgivable. Captive audience, right?

I don't want you to get the wrong picture. I enjoyed having conversations about Jesus with people, dipping below the surface small talk into the deep things of life. I wasn't forcing canned presentations on people. I wasn't a doomsday prophet standing on a street corner. But I always felt this inner compulsion, everywhere I went, a continual pressure to share my faith.

In one sense, this was a good thing. After all, we *should* expect to feel some desire to share our faith. If Christians really believe what Jesus taught—that a fiery eternity awaits unbelievers but eternal life is available to those who believe—then not sharing the rescuing grace of God with others is cruel. Atheist Penn Jillette of illusionist duo Penn and Teller frames this dilemma in stark terms:

> If you believe that there's a heaven and a hell, and people could be going to hell or not getting eternal life, and you think that it's not really worth telling them this because it would make it socially awkward ... how much do you have to hate somebody to *not* proselytize? How much do you have to hate somebody to believe everlasting life is possible and not tell them that?[4]

Did you catch the zinger at the end there? Penn points out that *not* sharing the gospel with others is tantamount to hate. Jesus clearly taught us to love our neighbor, the stranger, and even our enemy. And Paul says that "Christ's love compels us" to plead with others to be reconciled to God (2 Corinthians 5:14, 20 NIV). Even non-Christians understand this urgency. Consider the words of Ezra Koenig, front man of the band Vampire Weekend: "We know the fire awaits unbelievers ... Want a little grace but who's going to say a little grace for me?" [5] If the gospel is true, fire awaits unbelievers unless they receive grace. If Christians believe this, shouldn't we embrace the pressure to extend that grace to them? Isn't this pressure a good thing?

Well, yes and no. While it is good to want to share your faith, to tell others the good news about Jesus and what he has done for them, in many cases that pressure we feel to evangelize isn't good, especially when it drives us to manipulate others or to try to force a conversion.

PRESSURE EVANGELISM

Have you ever been on the other end of a "pressure sale"? A new insurance policy, refrigerator, car, or home, perhaps? How did it make you feel? You probably felt used, a means to an end. Or maybe you felt objectified, subhuman. You had the sense that the salesman didn't really care about you. He wasn't interested in your good—he just wanted to close the deal. That's how people sometimes feel when they are on the receiving end of our evangelistic efforts. They feel like they are a means to the end of *our* spiritual profit, like we are just trying to close a deal.

Several years ago, my wife worked in door-to-door sales for Yellow Book advertising. It was a miserable experience. Day after day, door after door, she was cussed out, mocked, and rejected. After three months of this, I told her to quit. I made it clear that we'd do whatever we had to do to scrape our living expenses together, but this job just wasn't worth the cost. Why was she so disliked by everyone? I can assure you it had nothing to do with her personally. My wife is a gregarious, joyful person and would have gotten along great with most of the people she was meeting, if the circumstances had been different. But she was soundly rejected, even hated, because everyone on the other side of the door was assuming a pressure sale. They immediately knew that they were a means to an end—and they despised it. They felt the pressure as soon as she opened her mouth, often cutting her off before she could even get started.

That's *exactly* how many people feel when we begin sharing our faith with them. The pressure we feel to share the gospel doesn't translate into the loving concern we may genuinely have for them. Instead, our compulsion bleeds through, coming across as a pressure sale, and people feel like a means to an end, a project. Even when what we say is true and we have good intentions, the way we say it can make people wish we weren't talking.

RELIEVING THE PRESSURE

So what's wrong with pressure evangelism? Just about everything. For starters, it reveals that we have the wrong motivation. When we talk with others, we aren't sharing out of a sense of freedom, loving others out of the overflow of our peace and contentment in Christ. We are evangelizing to prove ourselves out of a misguided sense that the eternal destiny of others is *ultimately* dependent on our efforts. In the end, it isn't love that compels us. The pressure to perform, to make the sale, presses down so hard on our hearts and minds that it distorts our message. We act and speak in unnatural ways. Often, we sound as if we don't really believe what we are saying. The gospel we share is *unbelievable.*

There are several, common ways of evangelizing that have been popular over the past few decades. My point in sharing these is not to disparage them or suggest they haven't been used by God. In fact, for each of these examples, the message is actually true in content, but disregards the context. As my Bible interpretation professor in seminary said, "Context is king." In most contexts today, evangelistic techniques tend to feel canned. In Evangelism Explosion, for example, you need to memorize an outline. With the Four Spiritual Laws you often end up reading from a tract and turning the pages. Most of these past efforts were focused on nailing a presentation, not on understanding a person. And this priority — to get the message out there and be heard — tends to make others feel like they are a project. To be fair, this was never the intended goal of these evangelistic tools, and I'm sure there are many people who are still able to use them effectively. But in my experience, the most common result is a canned presentation, one that doesn't really communicate God's good news in a *believable* way.

While I am deeply indebted to Campus Crusade for Christ (now Cru) for many things, I recoil at some of my evangelistic training. Eager to grow in my faith, I went on a summer project in Santa Cruz, California, where we rented the Peter Pan Motel for the summer. Fortunately, the staff arrived ahead of time to clean up the needles and condoms out of the rooms. What was a bastion of darkness, over the summer, was transformed into a beacon of light. I loved a lot of what we got to do, though I'll admit working for the Dipper Diner, in my polyester blue-and-white striped uniform, topped by a matching restaurant blue hat, was a bit humbling.

I think most of us feared the impending "Beach Evangelism" each time it rolled around. We were charged with creating a scene on the beach to "draw people in," and then, after cracking smiles with strangers, we were told to spin out and share the Four Spiritual Laws with them, taking them through the little paper tract tucked away in our back pocket. I reluctantly participated in our massive, attractional game of tug-of-war, but afterward just roamed the beach with my buddy. We connected with some folks playing beach volleyball, and we hung out with one guy in particular. Eventually the conversation turned to spiritual things. I kept the tract in my back pocket and just tried to relate Christ to what this guy was facing in life. Remarkably, he said he was interested in knowing Jesus and being rescued from his sins. We prayed with him as he repented and put his faith in Jesus. We encouraged him to get connected with a church and never saw him again. My buddy turned to me and said: "Man, I didn't know you could do that. You didn't even use the Four Spiritual Laws." I responded by saying, "If we had whipped out that tract, we would have lost the guy's attention right away."

Why do I share this story? Not to slam Cru. Like I said, I've learned a lot from them, evangelistic boldness in particular, and I even included my campus director, Jerry McCune, in the acknowledgments. I share this story to emphasize the point that evangelism doesn't have to be mechanical; it can be intuitive and relational. It doesn't have to be pressure-driven and event-oriented. Listening to people's stories, we can discern how to best share the gospel with them in a natural, relatable way. We don't have to fit an evangelistic mold.

While we can critique various approaches and methods, it isn't always the methods themselves that are to blame for pressure evangelism. We have a choice. Certain tools and trainings may create fertile soil for pressure evangelism, but its motivational roots run deep into our hearts, where we are preoccupied with what others think of us. Because we desire the approval of our spiritual mentors, our peers, and even God, we end up evangelizing to impress. We're like the teenager who works tremendously hard at a sport he doesn't even like, just to get the approval of his parents. We try to earn our acceptance by performing

Evangelism doesn't have to be mechanical; it can be intuitive and relational. It doesn't have to be pressure-driven and event-oriented. Listening to people's stories, we can discern how to best share the gospel with them in a natural, relatable way.

for the reward of approval. When we evangelize in this way, we are trying to earn the unearnable favor of the Father.

As a result, our gospel isn't believable. Why? Because our motivations don't line up with our beliefs. We aren't practicing what we preach. We may tell others that the Father loves them perfectly, that our salvation is based on Christ's performance and not our own, *and yet we are still motivated by a desire to earn God's favor.* As a church planter I was discouraged, in part because I wasn't measuring up to my own evangelistic standards. Instead of relying on God's sovereign grace, I felt the pressure to perform, to get higher numbers, to justify myself. If our church grew more rapidly through conversions, I could feel good about myself, about my performance. In these moments, my worth was slipping from the sure and treasured place of Christ, to the unwavering and idolatrous place of self. I preferred manufactured approval over the enduring approval of our heavenly Father.

When our evangelism is motivated by approval, "moments" of evangelistic opportunity devolve into something like this: "If I don't do this, I'm gonna regret it" (performance), instead of thinking, "I can see this person needs the hope of the gospel, and I can't wait to extend it" (love). The motivation of performance and the idol of approval short-circuit the motivation of love. Is it any surprise that people find our evangelism unbelievable? People are sacrificed on the altar of our efforts to gain God's approval through our performance.

The truth we need to hear and believe, at a deep heart level, is that God doesn't need you and me to accomplish his work. He doesn't want to use us in a manipulative, detached way. He wants to give himself to us. The apostles knew this in their bones. They knew they belonged to Christ. They knew they were deeply loved by the Father. They knew that regardless of what happened to them, their successes or failures, their future was secure. That's why the love of Christ compelled them. Paul mentions the compelling love of Christ to the Corinthian church, not just to clarify his motivations for evangelism, but to explain his motive for ministry. With his apostleship under fire, he grounds everything he does — all of this work and suffering — in the love of Jesus. He counts on only one thing in life and death: "that one has died for all, therefore all have died; and he died for all, that those who live might no longer live for themselves but for him who for their sake died and was raised" (2 Corinthians 5:14 – 15). The death and resurrection of Jesus wasn't merely his message; it was his motivation.

Paul was compelled to do all kinds of ministry in all sorts of circumstances, not to receive attaboys from God the Father, but because Jesus died to resurrect a whole new kind of humanity: "If anyone is in Christ, he is a new creation. The old has passed away; behold, the new has come" (2 Corinthians 5:17). Paul isn't performing; he's truly living. He is living a whole new life that revolves, not around self, but around the Messiah who died and lives for him. His evangelism is utterly Christ-centered.

When we are motivated by performance, we are self-centered, and we end up riddled with anxiety. Jesus died and rose from death to liberate us from this nasty way of living. The old is gone and the new has come. You are a new creation. Don't graduate from this. Sit in it and live in it. Tie your worth to the rock of Christ, crucified and risen. Train yourself to look at Christ and then at others with new eyes, until you too can see them becoming new. You are new — but there are lots of other people who aren't, for whom Jesus also died, and they don't know what it's like to be liberated from performance and a million other sins. Jesus died to liberate them too.

Our vision needs to be reshaped by the resurrection power of Jesus. In the resurrected Christ we get a glimpse of heaven overlapping earth. Paul tells us what this transformation did for him. He no longer saw people "according to the flesh," as numbers or objects to manipulate or to satisfy his own desires; rather, he saw them as potential recipients of God's new creation work. He saw sinners, not only for what they had done in their rebellion against God, but as people who could become the very righteousness of God *in Christ* (2 Corinthians 5:21).

It's not enough for us to simply see eternity in the balance; eternal math isn't enough to keep the evangelistic heart pumping. We must see Jesus, over and over again, as the source and goal of God's work, and we must look to him as the renewing power of new creation. Jesus is our motivation for evangelism, and the Father is calling us to count on Christ, more than anything else, and entrust our evangelistic record to him. Don't count on methods, conversions, cultural savvy, or your church. Count on Christ, deeply, and you will communicate Christ freely.

RETHINKING EVANGELISM

Before we move on, it's important we establish a working definition for evangelism. I like the definition by missiologist David Bosch: "Evangelism is: *the core, heart,* or *center* of mission: it consists in the proclamation of salvation in Christ to nonbelievers, in announcing forgiveness of sins, in calling people to repentance and faith in Christ, in inviting them to become living members of Christ's earthly community and to

Our vision needs to be reshaped by the resurrection power of Jesus. Paul no longer saw people "according to the flesh," as numbers or objects to manipulate or to satisfy his own desires; rather, he saw them as potential recipients of God's new creation work. He saw sinners, not for what they had done in their rebellion against God, but as people who could become the very righteousness of God *because of Jesus.*

"Evangelism is: *the core, heart,* or *center* of mission: it consists in the proclamation of salvation in Christ to nonbelievers, in announcing forgiveness of sins, in calling people to repentance and faith in Christ, in inviting them to become living members of Christ's earthly community and to begin a life in the power of the Spirit."
—*David Bosch*

begin a life in the power of the Spirit."[6] Note five distinct contributions in this definition. Evangelism: (1) is gospel-centered, (2) is proclamation oriented, (3) calls for a response, (4) includes the church, and (5) points to the Spirit.

Bosch's definition is *gospel-centered* in that it focuses on the person and work of Jesus Christ. It is not heaven-centered, like much of the evangelism of the twentieth century. The goal is Christ, not heaven.[7] It is *proclamation oriented*, unlike many deed-driven descriptions of evangelism. The gospel is good news to be shared, not good deeds to be observed, though it clearly issues into marvelous deeds of grace. Bosch also includes the importance of *calling for a response*, repentance and faith, as well as becoming a part of what we are converted into — *the church* — which is all too often overlooked in contemporary, individualistic evangelism. The church is not a loose collection of spiritually-minded individuals but a family knit together in the unshakable love of the Father. This is what we get and what the world needs to see. Finally, this definition inspiringly reminds us that our new life is not lived in our own power but *in the power of the Spirit*. Modern methods give lip service to the Spirit while 90 percent of training is aimed at the head. This definition gives us a clear target for evangelism. As the book unfolds, these five evangelistic distinctives will surface informally over and over again.

How, then, do we rethink our evangelism with these distinctives in view? New methods aren't enough. *Our whole understanding of evangelism needs to change — our motivations, our methods, and even our message.* The sections of this book broadly correspond to each of these, though there is some natural overlap and repetition. The first section, "Evangelistic Defeaters," addresses our motives and primarily focuses on our heart and mind — why we evangelize. The second section, "Re-Evangelization," addresses our message and what we communicate. The third section on "Gospel Metaphors" addresses our methods, primarily how we say what we say.

Defeaters	⇨	Motives	⇨	Heart and Mind
Re-evangelization	⇨	Message	⇨	Gospel
Gospel Metaphors	⇨	Methods	⇨	Speech

Our motives, message, and methods are all intertwined, pulling us together as humans on mission. If we take the time to untangle the strings, examining what is really there, pulling out a few threads that don't belong, and weaving in some new threads that are absent, we may end up not only with a reshaped evangelism but also with a revitalized Christian faith.

The gospel is central to how and why we evangelize. People need to see how the gospel speaks to their particular and unique needs. The gospel brings us exactly what we need: acceptance, approval, forgiveness, newness, healing, worth, purpose, joy, hope, peace, and freedom—all in Jesus. As we get started, we will begin by considering exactly why people find this gospel unbelievable. We need to pay attention to these evangelistic concerns and learn from them. Otherwise, we will perpetuate the distance between ourselves and those outside the faith. There are several obvious *evangelistic defeaters*—reasons why Christians often choose not to share their faith with others. Let's begin with the first of these defeaters—a genuine concern that our witness not be impersonal.

KEY QUESTIONS

1. What emotions or objections come to mind when you think about evangelism?
2. Can you identify with evangelistic failure? Share a story of your failure.
3. What do you do with "evangelistic pressure"?
4. What would change if you were compelled, not by pressure, but by the love of Christ?

01 DEFEATERS

This section is represented by an upside down triangle. This symbolizes the downward pull of the defeaters and the urgency of addressing them. Its depth reminds us that there are more defeaters to think through than are explained in this book.

It may seem strange to start a book on evangelism by focusing on reasons **not** to share the gospel. However, there are a couple important reasons for this. First, the cultural shift from formal presentational evangelism to informal relational evangelism has changed the questions everyday Christians ask themselves about sharing the gospel. This shift is reflective of a larger value shift from truth to community. Instead of asking, "What is the right thing to say?" many people are asking themselves, "What should I avoid saying?" When relationships are the primary value, not presentations, personal questions are naturally pushed to the surface. Second, when seismic cultural plates shift, friction erupts in the overlap of worldviews. The modern worldview, shaped by individual authority, reason, and practice, does not fit neatly into the postmodern worldview, which is shaped by community-formed authority, relativism, and experience.

As a result, people who are influenced by postmodernism find modernist evangelistic methods off-putting and ineffective. People who are more sensitive to relationships are quick to discern that rational, presentational approaches no longer work well within postmodern culture, where people want to be known, loved, and respected, not informed and presented to. Because of these cultural shifts and their impact on people, many have stopped sharing their faith. In fact, there has been a significant decline in evangelism among people between their thirties and fifties, who account for two out of every three active Christians today.[8] If we are going to experience a renaissance of evangelism, we must ask the question, "Why are these demographics less active in evangelism?" Instead of beating the evangelistic drum louder, we need to quiet down and listen to their evangelistic concerns. If we listen to these concerns, which I call defeaters, I believe we will gain greater wisdom for gospel communication in a whole new era.

By reflecting on these defeaters, you will have an opportunity to learn, adapt, and perhaps even repent. I certainly have. In considering each defeater, I have tried to look at them from two angles: Where is the defeater true, **and** how do we defeat the defeater? To put a point on it — this section is an exercise in cultural analysis for evangelistic wisdom. While it is not comprehensive, I hope it furnishes you with greater wisdom and discernment.

chapter two

IMPERSONAL WITNESS: RELATIONSHIPS, WORK, AND FAITH

As we emerged from the individualism of the late twentieth century to enter the swarming social media of the early twenty-first century, relationships have become a commodity. In his landmark book *Bowling Alone*, Robert Putnam documented the decline of relationships in the latter half of the twentieth century.[1] He notes that during this time:

- Attendance at *club meetings* fell 58 percent.
- *Family dinners* came down 33 percent.
- Having *friends visit* declined by 45 percent.

As the title of his book suggests, we are more likely to find someone "bowling alone" than with a club team. We haven't recovered from this decline. Today, social media has flooded in to fill the void left by our radical individualism.

How does the rise of social media affect our relationships? In a nod to Robert Putnam, Sherry Turkle's *Alone Together* argues that social media creates the illusion of companionship while leaving us isolated from one another.[2] We can have hundreds of Facebook friends, and thousands of Twitter followers, without having a single deep friendship. We share our thoughts with the world—posting our deepest feelings for all to see, but we may not have an actual person to listen to us. Our audience is a social network, not an actual friend in the flesh. The "friending" that occurs in social media is considered a weak social tie.[3] Putnam insists that true community is always localized, describing it as "a group of interacting people living *in a common location*."[4] While we can interact with those who live near to us online, an online community doesn't require us to be in a common location. There aren't the typical face-to-face interactions we necessarily have in real relationships where we work out the travails and joys of life together. Emoticons don't substitute for a real hug.

The habits we form online change the way we interact in person. For instance, we may "convo" all day long online, but be unable to carry an actual conversation very far. You may read a person's confessional blog and learn deep things about them, but when meeting them discover they can't or won't talk about these things in person. We are losing the *art of conversation*. Why? There are a number of factors, but we would be naive to think an online medium doesn't play a role. Online social interactions are often one-way monologues, not two-way dialogues. Despite commenting features, Facebook, Twitter, YouTube, and blogging are largely built on amplifying an individual's perspective, not genuine exchange. We extend the monologue into actual conversations, where we often end up "surfing" people for information instead of asking questions that take the conversation deeper. These shifts in the social landscape, from physical to digital, make deep relationships rare. This has a huge impact on evangelism. When it comes to talking about something as deep and personal as faith, we hesitate for fear of offending or losing a friend. We're on relational thin ice. Twenty-first-century Christians want people to know they are loved. Period. Without an evangelistic parenthesis.

THE EVANGELISTIC PROJECT

The relational climate affects the way we think about and engage in evangelism. Today, it is typical to get to know someone before talking with them about Jesus. We are more prone to talk about our work or family or to discuss music and movies. We keep our conversation in the realm of small talk before braving the mountains and valleys of deeper

The long onramp we
create to talk about
the gospel can be a
marvelous expression
of grace to others — a
"no" to the stereotype of
stiff proselytizing and a
"yes" to real, thoughtful
relationships.

truth. The long onramp we create to talking about the gospel can be a marvelous expression of grace to others—a "no" to the stereotype of stiff proselytizing and a "yes" to real, thoughtful relationships. We are slow to bring up the gospel with neighbors, acquaintances, and coworkers because we don't want people to feel like spiritual projects. This is especially true if we know someone who has been hurt or offended by impersonal evangelism.

Consider the consequences of an impersonal witness in our current cultural climate. The workplace evangelist, for example, can come across as impersonal and pushy. She campaigns for Jesus in the office without taking the time to really know people. Blinded by passion (and/or performance), she doesn't see what everyone else sees—a Christian looking to clear her evangelistic conscience. She treats people like projects and grades herself on how well she performs with them. Each project is graded on a check system:

- Not saying anything about Jesus earns a ✓-.
- Saying Jesus' name in conversation earns a ✓.
- Mentioning what Jesus did (on the cross, for your sins) earns a ✓+.
- Giving a "whole gospel presentation" earns a gold star. ★

This kind of evangelism is distasteful—and for good reason. It lacks the punch of authenticity and the flavor of credibility. It leverages people for spiritual worth. Name-drop Jesus, and we feel good. Wimp out and we feel bad. Enter the roller coaster of self-made spirituality, a far cry from Christ-centered faith. This evangelism is like social media, often more about us than it is for others. The checklist approach to evangelism fails to embody the truth of the message being communicated. While the gospel facts are present, their potency is absent. A checklist Christian eclipses the person of Christ. The impersonal evangelist is involved in a performance act. She performs as if God's favor hangs on her evangelistic obedience, when in reality Christ's obedience drapes us with the Father's favor. She blindly dismisses people's struggles, fears, hopes, and reasons for unbelief, moving down the list to get spiritual pats on the back. Her Christianity is answer-oriented, not heart-focused.

The film *The Big Kahuna*, starring Kevin Spacey and Danny Devito, takes place almost entirely in a hotel suite. On the last night of a convention, two senior lubricant salesmen and a junior protégé work tirelessly on their pitch for a big potential client—the big kahuna. As the story unfolds, the junior salesman, Bob, ends up hitting it off with the big potential client. As a result, Phil and Larry nervously coach him through what to say in the clutch meeting. When the time comes, Bob ends up spending hours with the big kahuna downstairs, while Phil and Larry pine away upstairs. Finally, after Bob returns, they tackle him with questions. Bob recounts how great the evening was, describing the depth of conversation, how much fun he had, and how important the night was, but when asked how the pitch went, he tells them that he ended up talking about Jesus instead. The ensuing dialogue is fascinating and could be analyzed for many insights. I will touch on a just a couple. When asked why he didn't pitch their lubricants, Bob insists that he was being honest with the man about his soul. Phil replies:

The question you have to ask yourself is, has it [honesty] touched the whole of my life? That means that you preaching Jesus is no different than Larry or anybody else preaching lubricants. It doesn't matter whether you're selling Jesus or Buddha or civil rights or how to make money in real estate with no money down. That doesn't make you a human being. It makes you a marketing rep. If you want to talk to someone honestly, as a human being ... ask him about his kids. Find out what his dreams are. Just to find out. For no other reason. Because as soon as you lay your hands on a conversation to steer it, it's not a conversation anymore. It's a pitch, and you're not a human being, you're a marketing rep.

Phil tells Bob that when he shares his faith in an impersonal way, he is no different than a marketing rep. He breaches matters of the soul with people he barely knows, never asking about their kids, listening to their dreams, or relating to them as fellow human beings. Sadly, this is a scathing, but all-too-true indictment of contemporary evangelism. When we are taught to engage in evangelism as a method or program, we move to Jesus in ways that are awkward, and it feels like a marketing move. Is there a better way?

Jesus taught us to love people first, and sharing our faith should be an expression of that love for our neighbor, not something separate from it. Jesus was the love of God incarnate, in the flesh. Let's consider Jesus' interactions with a wealthy, young man of significant social status who is seeking the answer to eternal life.[5] Jesus doesn't pounce on the seeker. He engages him. He asks him *questions* and tells a *story* (Luke 18:18–30). It all seems pretty casual. He engages the man's intellect, appealing to his understanding of good and his knowledge of the law. He treats him with dignity and converses in matters of personal interest to both of them. In the course of their conversation, the wealthy young man raises the perfect evangelistic question: "What must I do to inherit eternal life?" It's a great setup. How does Jesus respond to him? He avoids the fill-in-the-blank answer! Instead, he asks the man another question. Why? Is Jesus passing on a "perfect" opportunity to share the gospel?

Jesus responds with a question because he is interested in the heart, what truly drives the man, his inner motives and desires. Though the man is wealthy, Jesus sees the poverty of his life, and he wants to surface the things that are truly in the way of his happiness. To receive eternal life, this man needs more than just the right answer; he needs to abandon his idols, the false gods he has been trusting. But he doesn't see it; he is blind to his true condition. This is why Jesus tells him: "Sell all that you have and distribute to the poor, and you will have treasure in heaven; and come, follow me" (Luke 18:22). Why does Jesus tell him to *do* something for salvation instead of *believe* something? Isn't that contrary to the gospel of salvation by grace alone, through faith alone?

No. Jesus knows that by asking for the man's idol, he is asking for his heart. Jesus steers the conversation, but he steers it with love. He is more interested in the person, talking to him with care and wisdom, than he is in checking off another project.

Let's be honest. We are always steering conversations. The real question is: to what end? Jesus steers for the heart. What are you steering for?

HOW DO FAITH AND WORK RELATE?

Sometimes Christians, like Bob, use the workplace as a platform for evangelism. But if they aren't careful, they end up demeaning the work they do to advance the gospel. So how should our faith and work relate to one another? Is it possible to share our faith in the workplace, in a way that is respectful and honoring to God?

I'd love to get a hold of some of the furniture Jesus made as a carpenter. My guess is that it would be *excellent*. I doubt he would have etched a cross or an icthus on the back of the seat.[6] In Hebrews 11, the author of Hebrews tells us that Christians are people who have a conviction about things not seen (they have faith), and they act on these convictions (they work). Faith lets you see things that people without faith can't see, and as a result, *you live and work differently*.

Take Noah, for example: "By faith Noah, being warned by God

concerning events as yet unseen, in reverent fear constructed an ark for the saving of his household" (Hebrews 11:7). We read in Genesis that Noah knew about a coming flood, something that was "unseen" to his contemporaries. The world was in such a state of wickedness that God had promised Noah he was going to reboot his creation through a massive deluge. Though his sight told him otherwise, through the faculty of faith, Noah trusted and believed God. He heard and considered God's word, developed a conviction about it, and then took action in response. Noah had faith *and* he built an ark. Without faith, he would not have built the ark.

Now, let's take this one step further. Consider for a moment what would have happened if Noah had built a shoddy ark. What if he responded in faith to God's warning, but he decided to cut corners. His family would have drowned, along with the future of the entire human race. Noah's faith led him to do *good* work, to construct a well-made vessel, and that good work stood as a testimony to God's saving grace. There were no bumper stickers, no fish symbols on the trunk of the ark to testify to God. His life and work did that.

We need Christians who are willing to preach their faith *through* their work—people who, because of their faith in the unseen God, make God seen. Jesus puts it this way: "Let your light shine before others, so that they may see your good works and give glory to your Father who is in heaven" (Matthew 5:16). Jesus says that our good work will give public glory to God. It will draw the world's attention to him.

By faith Noah "constructed an ark." This wasn't any old ship. It was an unprecedented vessel, an act of cultural innovation. Up to this point in history, most boats were used for fishing, measuring no more than ten feet in length. They were typically made of skin, wood, and reeds. It wouldn't be until the Egyptian era that actual sailing vessels would be created. So Noah was building something that blew away cultural expectations. His ark was around 450 feet long, over one and a half football fields! It had multiple rooms, was lined with waterproof pitch, and made of solid wood. Shaped like a large rectangle, it carried the creatures that would populate a new creation. Noah was ahead of his time. His faith sparked cultural *innovation* for the glory of God's plan. So should ours.

Some might object to all of this by pointing out that God made a unique promise to Noah, one that he hasn't made to us. Let's consider that. Hasn't God promised you and me that he will bear our judgment by rescuing us on a wooden cross and grant us new humanity in a new creation? Hebrews 11 says as much, connecting the faith of Noah to our faith as believers in Jesus Christ: "These all died in faith, not having received the things promised, but having seen them and greeted them from afar ... they desire a better country ... for [God] has prepared for them a city" (Hebrews 11:13, 16). Noah's faith in God profoundly affected his work.

We know that in the days after Noah, humanity fell back into rebellion. Noah did not see or experience the new humanity. He didn't find the better country that God had promised, the new creation. But we have been given a taste of it. If you are in Christ, the old person is gone and the new person has come through the gift of the Holy Spirit. Jesus is the better Noah, the one who survives the flood of God's judgment to resurrect a new humanity and usher in the new city, the city of God. Do you have faith in Christ? If so, you have even more reason than Noah to work with excellence and innovation. You are a citizen of the coming city, where culture making abounds. Are you working out your faith? Is your faith producing works that honor God and bless others?

Dorothy Sayers describes work as "the gracious expression of creative energy in the service of others."[7] Christian work should be excellent and innovative. We should always seek to improve, to bless, and to serve others through our work. A first step could be as simple as brightening your office with flowers or being faithful with your hours. But we should add to this reliable, competent work. In his helpful book *Every Good Endeavor*, Tim Keller recounts the story of a faithful and competent airline pilot landing in an emergency.[8] When you are flying, what matters most to you — that the pilot is a Christian or that the pilot is an excellent pilot? We shouldn't have to choose. Christians should be "excellent pilots" because of their devotion to Jesus. By faith we work,

How we work tells people what we *see.*

and our work should cause our coworkers and customers to give glory to our Father who is in heaven. The work we do isn't a platform for sharing spiritual platitudes; it is the proof of our faith working through love. How we work tells people what we *see.*

If we want to make much of Jesus, we will draw attention to him not only in what we say but also in what we do. Christians who demean their vocation in the name of evangelism misrepresent Christ himself. They distort his message. The best way to remedy this is by participating in the whole gospel, a story that narrates redemption for *all creation.*

HOW MUCH OF THE GOSPEL DO WE NEED TO SHARE?

Our work is a witness. What we do and how we do it communicates something about us—what we believe and what we value. But while our work says something, it doesn't say everything. The Bible is clear that faith comes by hearing, by hearing the word of Christ. What is the "word of Christ"? How do we know if we are sharing this word? Are there key doctrines we need to cover to know if someone has been truly evangelized?

Let's consider another conversation Jesus had. On another occasion an expert in the law approached Jesus and asked him a question, one similar to the question the rich young man asked him: "What shall I do to inherit eternal life?" Jesus gets a "second chance" at a perfect setup! Surely he won't miss this one. Today, you'd expect Jesus to take him through the Roman Road, move through the Four Spiritual Laws, maybe even show him the Two Ways to Live, then close the deal by asking him to pray a prayer.[9] Obviously, Jesus doesn't do this, but what's most striking is that *initially he doesn't even answer the question.*

By contemporary standards, Jesus blows his evangelistic opportunities. Instead of trying to obtain the right confession, Jesus focused his words on the heart.

What does Jesus do? He responds, again, by asking the expert in the law several questions. Why? Why does Jesus turn down a great opportunity to teach, to explain, to make everything clear and obvious? Because Jesus knows that answers are not enough. He knows that there is another "god" reigning in the lawyer's heart, one that has to be removed before it can be replaced. So he asks questions to meet the lawyer where he is. He asks questions to expose where he finds his true worth: "What is written in the Law? How do you read it?" (Luke 10:26). Jesus isn't dismissive of the lawyer's knowledge of the law; on the contrary, he engages it. Jesus knows more than the lawyer and could have probably given him a fifty-minute lecture on the topic. Instead, he respects him and meets him where he is. He steers toward the heart by addressing what is most important to the lawyer, the law.

There is a time and place for discussing questions and objections. Being personal doesn't mean avoiding a skeptic's objections to the Bible. It doesn't mean talking about family and pop culture while avoiding intellectual discussions of the faith. It means learning what matters to a person, trying to understand how it is important to them, and gently exposing their deeply held beliefs and desires. After hearing the lawyer's response, Jesus affirms his answer: "You have answered correctly; do this, and you will live" (Luke 10:28).

We can learn from this answer as well. There is great power in affirmation. It's in rare supply today. We all want it but few give it. Take time to encourage people, affirming the things that are good and true as you talk with them about life. Affirm their good desires, their thoughtful skepticism, their sincere objections, and their truthful answers. When non-Christians speak up in our City Group gatherings, they often have very good insights into the Scriptures and life. One evening a recently divorced woman was sharing how she battled through her ex-husband's inflexibility and meanness. She shared, "I am learning not to put my trust in people but to put my trust in God." What a massive insight, a life-changing truth! Faith in God, and not in people, enables us to suffer well. I affirmed her right there, on the spot: "Andrea, that is such an important truth, and one we all need to hear. I know that's a difficult lesson you are learning right now, but I want to encourage you to keep leaning into it."

After Jesus affirms the lawyer, the conversation isn't over. The lawyer wants to prove himself right, so he asks Jesus another question: "And who is my neighbor?" Jesus responds, not with a statement or by quoting a Bible verse, but by telling him a story. This is genius. Stories open us up to alternative perspectives because they trigger our imagination, the creative side of our brain. This is why C. S. Lewis, in addition to writing apologetics works like *Mere Christianity* and *The Problem of Pain*, also began writing science fiction and the well-known fantasy series, the Chronicles of Narnia.[10] As Westerners, who put more value on argumentation, we would expect Lewis's career to begin with stories and mature into apologetics, but it was deliberately the opposite. Lewis once wrote: "The more imaginative a mythology, the greater its ability to communicate more Reality to us."[11]

So Jesus, wisely, uses a story to answer the lawyer's question. He imagines a story about a merciful Samaritan, someone who would have been culturally despised, who shows more compassion to a mugging victim than a respectable Jewish priest or an honored Levite. Jesus concludes the story by asking the expert in Jewish law: "Which person do you think proved to be a neighbor?" The story made it obvious. There was only one answer. The Samaritan was clearly the neighbor. The Jewish expert was left with the inescapable truth that acts motivated by a heart of mercy are greater proof of love than the status or beliefs a person holds. Jesus then gives the lawyer a challenge: "You go, and do likewise" (Luke 10:37).

Through this story, Jesus surfaces the deep idol of the lawyer's heart—his knowledge of the law. Jesus shows that the lawyer's self-righteous intellect was keeping him from being compassionate, especially toward those of a hated socio-ethnic class. Jesus could have said this to him directly. He could have called him to repent and trust God, but he didn't. Jesus didn't even tell the lawyer what to believe; he told him what to do. Then he used the story to help the man see what he was unwilling to see, his own need for a Savior.

I am not a natural storyteller. I have to work at telling a story. But I do have stories I can tell, stories of how God has provided for me, how his promises have gotten me through a hard time, how his people are a source of encouragement, how I was moved by a psalm I read or a song I sang with my community. I repeat some stories. Countless times, I've shared how God provided our home through unexpected generosity. Many times I've shared how my daughter's eye was healed after I stopped praying just for her good and began praying she would be healed for God's glory. When that happened, I was able to tell my gay neighbor friend about it and implicitly point him to God's power and grace. My personal stories of struggle, failure, and suffering are among the most effective. In these stories, we become human and the gospel becomes divine. We all love stories; we just need to work a bit at seeing Christ in the middle of them and retelling them to help and bless others.

What can we learn from Jesus about engaging in evangelism that is believable, that is honest and true, that gets to the heart? So far, we have learned several things.

BELIEVABLE EVANGELISM

1. Ask questions; it isn't just about giving answers.
2. Focus on the heart, not just on the mind.
3. Steer conversation, with love and wisdom, toward deeply held beliefs and desires.
4. Value and affirm the insights of skeptics and seekers.
5. Tell stories from — and to — the heart.

You'll see these important practices surface throughout the rest of the book. Is there one you need to work on? If you can pick one now, you can begin growing in believable evangelism right away.

It's clear that sharing the gospel is important, but how much of the gospel should we share? After all, Jesus himself didn't cover half the material most evangelicals are expected to cover. I suggest we keep a couple things in mind. *First, good evangelism isn't an all-or-nothing endeavor.* While we should learn to state clearly the truth that Jesus died for our sins on a cross, in our place; that he took on himself the consequences of our sin and conquered it, death, and evil, by rising again to new life; that he offers us forgiveness through repentance and faith in him; and that he promises a whole new world — *this can come in bits and pieces.* As we've noticed in the ministry of Jesus, the goal in evangelism isn't merely to get a gospel presentation out in one breath! The goal is to get to the heart, and that might not happen the first time you meet someone.

Jesus asked questions, he told stories, and he was a master at getting to the inner longings and desires of people. He knew that providing the right answer wasn't enough. At the same time, Jesus didn't avoid the truth. He spoke about mercy, the law, and loving God and neighbor. His conversations were theological, but they weren't formulaic. He was willing to hear out the lawyer's counterpoints and objections. Too often Christians insist on getting their views across, committed to getting out a gospel presentation instead of really communicating with a person.

Once our message is communicated, we judge our effectiveness by visible response instead of trusting that God is always at work and that we simply get to join him in talking with people about the deepest, most meaningful truths of life. If nothing happens, we move on, wiping our hands clean: "Evangelism, check!"

This isn't evangelism. It certainly isn't believable. People need something more credible than sound bites and an experience more meaningful than being treated like a project. We need to turn away from the checklist and turn to the people in front of us. Don't worry about sharing a predetermined gospel statement. Don't worry if you don't strike every point from your evangelistic training. God isn't looking for us to cover a set number of doctrines. You can even have a conversation with a non-Christian and not share the "gospel," and God won't think less of you. Commenting on Luke 10:25–37, Jerram Barrs asks: "Do we trust the Lord enough to send someone away without telling the person how to inherit eternal life?"[12] What are you trusting? God or a single, point-in-time presentation? Put your faith in God, not in your evangelism. God can even use your lack of knowledge as a way of beginning a conversation with a non-Christian. Invite them to explore a question further with you; consider their doubts and deepen your faith. You might just learn together.

The second thing to bear in mind regarding how much of the gospel we need to share in a conversation is this: *good evangelism takes time.* If we are sharing the gospel in bits and pieces, getting to know a person and their hopes and fears, talking about faith in one conversation, sin in another, and then Christ three conversations after that, all of this is going to take time. Getting to the heart is a process, not a one-time event. We need what Michael Frost calls in his second chapter "Slow Evangelism."[13] He writes:

> Part of the problem with evangelism is many Christians feel they need to get the whole gospel out in one conversation. The reason for this is many Christians are only ever in a position to "evangelize" strangers, because all their friends are Christians ... Evangelizing friends and neighbors, gradually, relationally, over an

extended time, means that the breadth and beauty of the gospel can be expressed slowly without the urgency of the one-off pitch.

You don't have to get the entire gospel out — covering every nuance — in one conversation. Yes. The pressure is off! Author and pastor Hugh Halter even goes so far as to recommend *not* witnessing to someone until you've known, loved, and served them for a year.[14] This may not be true in every situation, but given our current cultural context and the suspicions and stereotypes people have about evangelism, it makes sense. Develop rich relationships, share life, eat meals with neighbors, go to the movies, hang out at home, go to a happy hour with a coworker, and *love* your neighbors, coworkers, and non-Christian friends. Jesus did. Start with casual conversation. Ask questions. Get to know them. Over time, you may be invited to talk about real issues in their lives where you can share a gospel worth believing. Or you may gain insight into their idolatry and have an opportunity to apply the gospel to that area of their life in order to guide them more clearly to Christ. Until then, you may need to slow down and learn to love and enjoy others first.

We too need the gospel. We need to think about what we believe and allow the gospel to work itself into our own life, our ideas, our dreams, and our desires. When we do, our faith will begin to come out naturally in our work and in our love for people. When we slow down, the gospel becomes more than a message we repeat — it becomes a conviction that ravishes our heart. The gospel not only saves us; it changes us. Where is the gospel changing you? Challenging you? Convicting you? Encouraging you? What would it look like if you began to share that with others? One of the best things you can do is authentically to share your need for the gospel with others. I call this *sharing the gospel with yourself out loud*.

Share the gospel with yourself *out loud*.

It was one of our regular nights at the Gingerman pub. Dave and I had just finished up a pretty philosophical conversation. It started to rain outside, so we moved inside. Once we got situated, Dave looked at me and said, "Jon, do you ever doubt?" It's funny how people can build up an impossible version of you in their minds. I replied: "Well, it depends on what you mean by doubt. I don't doubt the basic claims of Christ, but I do struggle with unbelief." Dave glanced at me with a puzzled look on his face. For example, earlier today I posted something on Twitter that I thought was pretty insightful. I checked an hour later and no one had re-tweeted it. I checked again, and still, no comment. Then again, no star, no tweet, nothing. My heart sank. Why? Because I believed the approval of the anonymous Twittersphere was more valuable than the approval of God in Christ. I disbelieved that Jesus is better than Twitter. The more we reveal our own need for the gospel, the clearer the gospel will become. However, if we aren't fighting to believe that Jesus is better, it will be hard to do this — to be authentically Christian.

As you slow down, listen closely to what people really believe; listen for the desire beneath the words. Where appropriate, ask questions like: How does that make you feel? What do you really want? If you could change the circumstances to fit exactly what you want, what would it be? Look for trigger words that indicate fear, joy, anxiety, hope, despair, concern, and anger. Then, think about how Christ intersects that need. When you do this, you'll find that the gospel says something that the person will find worth believing. I'll share a lot of these examples in part 3. For now, be encouraged that the gospel is a rich reservoir you can draw from, and it speaks to the diverse desires of human beings across cultures and generations.

For many people today, hearing that Jesus died on the cross for their sins is entirely irrelevant. It is an abstract concept that doesn't connect with the heart. It's our job to show them how it does. When we speak to people's deepest desires, dreams, hopes, fears, or longings, we make the gospel believable. We get to show them more than a proposition; we get to show them the person of Jesus and the difference he makes. When we get in this deep with people, our evangelism will be far from impersonal. However, if evangelism is just a project or a program, we

When Francis Schaeffer was asked what he would do if he had an hour with a non-Christian, he replied by saying he would listen for fifty-five minutes. Then, in those last five minutes, he would have something to say.

aren't likely to get close enough to people to apply the good news to their heart, the place they truly believe.

It may be helpful to consider Francis Schaeffer's advice on this matter. When asked what he would do if he had an hour with a non-Christian, he replied by saying he would listen for fifty-five minutes. Then, in those last five minutes, he would have something to say.[15] To take it a step further, even if you don't say a gospel proposition in those last five minutes—that's okay! You can listen and pray, perhaps tell a story of God's work in your own life, empathize with their struggle, or offer to pray with them on the spot. Moderate your pace. The gospel isn't just a message we speak, checking off our list of things to do. It's a creative word, a seed that must be scattered and watered by many people over time, with prayer, grace, and love, until it germinates in good soil, producing fruit that leads to eternal life. Sow generously, be patient, and trust the results to God.

KEY QUESTIONS

1. Do you struggle to go deep in conversations? Why do you think this is so?
2. Do you see a disconnect between your social media and everyday speech?
3. How does *The Big Kahuna* movie show evangelism gone bad? Gone good?
4. What would have happened to humanity if Noah built a shoddy ark?
5. Where does your approach to work need to change?
6. What is one area where is God changing you? How can you apply the gospel to yourself out loud in conversation with others?

chapter three

PREACHY WITNESS:
SELF-RIGHTEOUS PROSELYTIZING

Another reason people find it difficult to share their faith is because they don't want to be seen as being "preachy." What does it mean to be preachy? Think of snarky, self-righteous Angela from *The Office*. Quick to judge everyone at work, she jumps on every opportunity to be right and show everyone else they are wrong. In one episode, Angela snaps at a remark her coworker Pam makes about needing more "loaves and fishes"—a way of suggesting that they need more food for a work party. Instead of making the effort to understand, Angela retorts with sarcasm: "Jesus is not your caterer." Thanks for the clarification, Angela. She comes across as spiritually superior, and beneath her self-righteous attitude lurks a deep hypocrisy. If you've watched the show, you know that Angela sleeps with Dwight and cheats on him with another coworker, Andy. She does all of this as a self-proclaimed Christian. Angela comes across as the last thing a disciple of Jesus should want to be—preachy and hypocritical—and yet sadly, she is not unique. We can all probably tell stories about "those Christians" we've met who are glaring hypocrites.

The film *Saved!* offers up another example of preachy witness in Mandy Moore's character, Hilary Faye, who exposes another layer of "preachy," self-righteous witness. She forms a "Christian Jewel" club

Instead of repelling sinners and seekers, Jesus' holiness brought him scandalously close to skeptics, prostitutes, and social rejects.

with her holy roller friends, which excludes and judges anyone who isn't a Christian or up to her moral standards. Her repeated attempts to convert others continually fail. She even tries exorcising a demon out of her drifting Christian (and secretly pregnant) girlfriend, Mary, who is struggling with guilt over having premarital sex. Frustrated her exorcism doesn't work, she yells at Mary, throwing the Bible at her, screaming: "I am filled with the love of Christ!" Until Hilary's self-righteousness is exposed, she doesn't grasp her deep need for the love of Christ. This is the popular impression of Christianity—insular, self-righteous, and hypocritical. Self-righteousness, passed off as holiness, is one of the greatest obstacles to people hearing a loving, grace-filled gospel. Instead of repelling sinners and seekers, Jesus' holiness brought him scandalously close to skeptics, prostitutes, and social rejects.[1] It didn't drive them away.

Because the "preachy Christian" is a stereotype many in our culture are familiar with—and strongly dislike—we are often hesitant to bring up spiritual matters in our conversations for fear of being perceived as self-righteous. As a student, I remember walking through the free speech area at the University of North Texas, cringing as I heard the fundamentalist yellers spew hate and judgment, with a little bit of Jesus thrown in. They stood on a box to yell, looking down on the rest of us, sounding off with hell, fire, and damnation. I did my best to correct this impression of Christianity with my non-Christian friends on campus. After Ancient Philosophy class, we would head over to Cool Beans bar on Fry Street to discuss life and faith over drinks. My friends would never have warmed to preachy self-righteousness, but they were open to dialogue in a setting where they could share their own thoughts and opinions. They admitted that our times together undid many of their presuppositions about Christians.

Street preachers aren't the only people who are self-righteous. We all have a bit of self-righteousness in us. If we're honest, there are people who we think aren't worth our time; perhaps they are even beyond being saved. Self-righteousness isn't just a turn-off; it's the opposite of the gospel. It communicates salvation through pious living, not through faith in Jesus' perfect, better-than-all life. Preachy self-righteousness says: "If you perform well (morally or spiritually), God will accept you." But the gospel says, "God already accepts you because Jesus performed perfectly on your behalf." There's a huge difference between these two! The gospel sets us free from performance and releases us into the arms of Christ. Self-wrought performance is a death sentence, but the obedience of Christ on our behalf is eternal life. The difference is grace. People need to hear grace: audacious, seems-too-good-to-be-true but so-true-it's-good, grace.

True grace moves downward, from God to us. God is opposed to the proud (up), but he gives grace to the humble (down). Grace is God working his way down to us so that we don't have to work our way up to him. And God comes down to us in Jesus. When we place our spirituality, morality, theology, politics, or anything else in front of the gospel, it creates a stumbling block in the way to Jesus. People will trip over our blocks, mistaking our better-than-thou witness for gospel truth. We need to clear away the blocks, turn the tables, and make grace the stumbling block, not our preachy self-righteousness or spiritual performance. The only thing we should put between our relationships with others is Jesus. This testifies to a more believable gospel, but a preachy witness testifies to an unbelievable gospel.

EVANGELISM IS NOT PROSELYTIZING

How do we remove these stumbling blocks to clear the way to Christ? Clarifying terms is always a helpful first step. Let's begin by making a distinction between proselytizing and evangelism.[2] A preachy witness is a form of proselytizing, which is quite different from the biblical definition of evangelism, the announcement of God's good news. Pope Francis's recent comments condemning proselytizing have puzzled many Catholics, particularly while openly calling Catholic believers to increase their evangelism. A closer examination of his statements, however, reveals that Pope Francis is not making a contradiction; rather, he is distinguishing between proselytizing and evangelism. He insists that proselytizing builds walls, while evangelism builds bridges.[3] Why? Because proselytizing is motivated by recruitment. Those who proselytize try to recruit people to their team. A proselytizer puts his faith in rational arguments or social networks. He thinks to himself, "If I can just disprove my coworkers' belief system and expose them to a lot of people who share my beliefs, they will be swept into Christianity." He might not be consciously aware that he is doing this, but those who think this way are acting like spiritual recruiters. While we should all be on God's mission, God hasn't called us to be recruiters for his team.

The problem with being a spiritual recruiter is that we often enlist people into the wrong things. We recruit to what we are really into, what we think is most important. Some focus on a political party, or a moral code, or a view of the book of Revelation. Others try to recruit to a particular form or denomination of church, or a doctrinal stance. *None of these is about Jesus.*

When we are recruiting, we end up sharing a false gospel, one that goes something like this: "If you join the right church and learn the right doctrines, then you can be saved." The proselytizer's good news is that you can swap out your inferior beliefs and community for her superior beliefs and better community. This approach demeans people who have strong friendships and sincere beliefs; more disturbingly, it points them to faith in a false god. It teaches people to trust in believing the right things and joining the right church.

Harvard religion professor Harvey Cox makes a helpful distinction between belief and faith when he says: "We can *believe* something to be true without it making much difference to us, but we place our *faith* only in something that is vital for the way we live."[4] Anyone can believe doctrines without changing their lives, but when we put our faith in Jesus, we are acknowledging that he is vital to our life, like oxygen is to the body. Proselytizing settles for doctrinal belief, but evangelism calls people to vital faith. Recruiting people to your church is also insufficient. The church isn't meant to bear the weight of our spiritual hunger for security and relational connectedness; only God can do that—Father, Son, and Spirit.

In contrast to proselytizers, who act as spiritual recruiters for God, evangelists are announcers. We announce the good news of grace, alert people to the promise of forgiveness, and share the hope of new life. As emissaries of King Jesus, we simply spread the saving word of his kingdom. We show people where it is, and how to enter it—through Jesus. As ambassadors, we realize we have neither the power nor the responsibility to change people. We cannot recruit them into the kingdom. Proselytizing, by contrast, replaces emissaries with enforcers and ambassadors with soldiers. It tries to force people into the kingdom, which feels more like works and less like grace. It places faith in human effort, not in divine intervention. When we proselytize, we assume we have both the power and the responsibility to talk people into the kingdom of God. We sideline the Holy Spirit in the search for conversions. Instead of making Jesus the focus of the gospel, recruiters zoom in on other things. Paul had strong words for Peter when he lost his Jesus focus, charging him with not walking in step with the gospel (Galatians 1:6–10; 2:11–14). When we are in step with the Spirit, we reflect the good news. Evangelists share the hope of faith in Jesus. Proselytizers share faith, but not faith in Jesus.

RESHAPING EVANGELISM

With the motivational issues of proselytizing laid bare, does this mean we must somehow get our motivations perfect before sharing the gospel? No. We will never be flawless in our motivations. Recall that even

Paul rejoiced when Christ was preached from selfish ambition, from deceptive motives (Philippians 1:17 – 18). Everyone fluctuates in their motivations for evangelism from time to time.

Recently, several women in our church were discipling a skeptical molecular biologist named Doreen. Doreen was a divorced mother with thoughtful objections to the gospel, and she had a rough past with the church. She was endeared by our ladies, and eventually by the larger church community. Eventually Doreen showed more interest in Christ and began reading the Scriptures and sharing meals with others. It was wonderful to see her taking steps to grow in her faith.

Then, for whatever reason, she slowly started to slip away. Doreen eventually came to the point where she confessed to loving Jesus for his sacrifice and forgiveness but rejected the idea that he rose from the dead.[5] Doreen eventually wrote her community group a letter explaining that she needed to move on from the church, despite her great love for the friendships there, to join a more liberal church that suited her theology and views. The community group struggled with this, but finally came to repent of putting more trust in their evangelistic efforts than in Christ himself. Amidst their genuine love lay tainted motives for evangelism — to prove to themselves they were a truly "missional" community. Losing Doreen was difficult for them, but through this experience they learned to put their faith in God's wise providence, not in their own evangelistic efforts. They renewed their focus, not on doing a better job in sharing their faith, but by turning to a better Savior, who forgave and reinvigorated them to continue on in his mission. Their act of repentance realigned them with Christ and restored their motives to love Doreen, brightening their witness.

A reshaped evangelism has to begin with reshaped motives and a heart of personal repentance. This will ensure that it is Christ who is cherished and Christ who is shared. We need to reflect honestly on our motivations for evangelism; are we counting converts or counting Christ? As you can see, having the wrong motivation for witnessing can distort our evangelistic methods, which in turn distorts our gospel message. As a result, evangelistic motivations, methods, and even the message can all get bent.

CHANGING THE "PREACHY" PERCEPTION

So how do we avoid being perceived as preachy and self-righteous? By returning to the gospel and believing it ourselves. The gospel reminds us that we don't have what it takes to stand before a holy God, that Christ alone has what it takes, and that he died and rose to give that to us. The gospel is offensive to our self-righteousness. It lifts up a mirror to show us who we really are, which can be disturbing. But the gospel is also redemptive; it lifts up Christ to show us who we have and can become.

Another way to change the preachy perception is to let our actions do the preaching. If we present the world with a kinder and quieter Christian, won't that solve the problem? Consider the quote often misattributed to St. Francis, "Preach the gospel at all times, and when necessary use words." Truth be told, St. Francis was an avid preacher of the gospel and didn't say this at all.[6] The gospel is good news to be shared, not good deeds to be observed, though it issues in marvelous deeds of grace. Doing good things may genuinely help others in need, but no one is going to look at your deeds and conclude: "I must be a sinner in need of God's grace. I need to repent of trusting in myself and others, and turn to Christ alone for forgiveness, and trust in him for redemption and acceptance before a holy God."

Actions are important, but they don't articulate. When Christians

The gospel is offensive; it lifts up a mirror to show us who we really are. But it is also redemptive; it lifts up Christ to show us who we have and can become.

press mute on the gospel, people are left to make up their own version of the good news. As a result, other religions and spiritualities are perceived as equally capable of giving them the good life. We wrongly think our silence will remedy the perception of self-righteousness, but in the end it still communicates it, just in another form: "Do good and you too can become a Christian."

One morning I was having a congenial chat with an Asian businessman in Starbucks. When he asked me what I was doing, I responded, "I'm working on a sermon." He immediately replied by waving his hands, one across the other. "Oh, no," he said. "I don't want to hear the sermon. Don't preach to me! Don't preach to me!" His exclamation was followed by a nervous chuckle. He perceived preaching as self-righteous judgment.

What would you say in response to him? I remember just brushing it off, saying something like, "No problem ... don't worry about that." I quieted down to avoid the preachy perception, but as a result, I left him with the wrong impression of Christianity. I should have immediately let him know that he had nothing to fear because true gospel preaching doesn't mound up guilt; it relieves guilt. Good preaching doesn't just show you your sins, it shows you a Savior, who absorbs your sins in his death and presents you to a holy God, cleaned up and new. Gospel preaching is meant to relieve your woes and remove your guilt through faith in Jesus.

So how do we correct this incorrect view of the gospel? Only words can clarify the meaning of the gospel. Paul remarks: "And how are they to believe in him of whom they have never heard? And how are they to

When Christians press mute on the gospel, people are left to make up their own version of the good news.

People won't be able to get past preachy images of religion unless someone "preaches" a message of grace to them.

hear without someone preaching?" (Romans 10:14). Our neighbors need to hear, and we need to preach. People won't be able to get past preachy images of religion unless someone "preaches" a message of grace to them.

Ministering in Austin, I spend a lot of time with people who have progressive views. My wife and I befriended a couple. The wife believed "the universe has an answer" to her problems. The husband was an actor down on his luck without any religious commitments. As we spent time together over dinner, at birthday parties, neighborhood gatherings, and just doing life, the husband, Steve, began to show interest in Christianity. We had several lunches together discussing spiritual things. He struggled with believing that Jesus is the divine Son of God, so we spent some time talking through this.

As all of this was happening, he and his family got more and more involved in our church. He ran sound, listened to sermons, read my books, and even participated in a small group. Looking at him from the outside, you would think he had changed his beliefs and was now a new Christian. After all, how could someone plunge waist deep into gospel community without actually believing the gospel? I was naturally curious to hear how this change had happened, so I arranged to meet him for lunch. I asked him, "How are things with Jesus?" He proceeded to tell me about some struggles at work with a "moral superior," and then told me that "he was having a hard time climbing the spiritual ladder."

After asking questions, it was clear to me that he didn't understand the gospel of grace. Had he been sleeping through my sermons? Through this experience, I came to see that secular people can be involved in church, change their behaviors and lingo, and actually become *religious*. Surprisingly, it isn't all that hard for someone to mistake clear gospel preaching with moral, religious teaching. People tend to hear what they want to hear, confirming what they already believe. This is why gospel preaching and teaching, as good as they are, are not enough. We need everyday evangelists, people who are willing to rub shoulders with those outside the church, hang out at their parties, take them to lunch, and ask enough loving questions to surface true beliefs. It takes time, conversations, and patience for people to get grace, to get it down into their hearts.

I'm not sure where Steve got the impression that Jesus died and rose to help us with moral and spiritual ladder climbing.[7] But his story reminds me that it's not enough to talk to people about Jesus; we need gritty gospel conversations, the give and take of asking questions and listening to what people really believe. Religion is in our hearts; it's in

Secular people can be very religious. Eager to excel, they may transpose their performance mentality onto the gospel. The only way to know when this happens is by asking questions that surface their true beliefs.

the air we breathe. The desire to excel at spiritual performance knows no boundaries; it crosses into all religions and philosophies. It's the prideful belief that somehow, by some way, we can actually prove ourselves good enough, worthy enough for salvation and praise. Good evangelism is getting to know people well enough to sense where that religious impulse is at work in their heart, and then clearly offering them an exchange—their works for Christ's work.

Being a preachy proselytizer is an obstacle to the gospel. It's not enough for us to just "preach the gospel." Christians also need to dismantle stereotypes and communicate alternative understandings of the faith by living in step with the Spirit and bearing his fruit of love, joy, peace, patience, kindness, goodness, gentleness, and self-control (Galatians 5:22–23). Our sanctification is part of our mission, but it is not the message itself. Godly character and social service are helpful in changing perceptions of Christianity, but they are never enough, in themselves, to save. Silent virtue and social justice can't replace the good news of the gospel. People won't intuitively know that grace flows down through the life and death of Jesus on their behalf. They will continue to believe that salvation is something you work toward, something you climb up. That's why they need to hear the gospel of God working down to them in Jesus, rescuing them from the darkness and placing them in his kingdom of light (Colossians 1:14).

KEY QUESTIONS

1. How have you encountered preachy Christianity? Do you think God uses it? If so, what's wrong with it?
2. What stumbling blocks do you tend to put in front of the gospel (political, moral, theological, cultural)?
3. How is evangelism different from proselytizing?
4. Why does mere critique of preachy evangelism fall short?

chapter four

INTOLERANT WITNESS: NAVIGATING PLURALISM

It was a typical night at the Gingerman, a low-lit, wood-paneled, leather-chaired pub in the heart of the city. I often meet here with people to talk and enjoy their company. Dave and I were there on a cool, autumn evening. We passed the crowds of people, walking the length of the bar and heading outside to the open-air beer garden. There we found a perfect spot — remote and unoccupied in the midst of a maze of communal wooden tables. Dave is a classically trained cellist, a member of an alt rock band, and prone to pondering the deep things of life. Since I love music and deep conversation, we are good friends.

Occasionally Dave will pepper me with random spiritual questions. "What about Jesus in India, Jon?" (Only Dave calls me Jon.) I respond to his question with a question of my own: "What about Jesus in India, Dave?" He explains. "You know, there are reports that Jesus appeared over there, reports *that aren't in the Gospels*. What do you make of that?" We've been talking about whether or not the Gospels of the New Testament are reliable. As we talk, I suggest that while it is possible that Jesus could have appeared in India, the real question is whether it's probable. After all, there is no record of it anywhere.[1] What we do know is that the church in southern India started after St. Thomas took the gospel there. It's called the Mar Thoma church, named after the apostle Thomas. If

Jesus had appeared in India, apart from the preaching of the apostles, isn't it probable that there would be a record of it? And wouldn't they have named the church after Jesus? Dave asked me several more questions. He made several interesting points about Eastern religions, and our conversation quickly moved to the exclusivity of Christianity.

At this point, Dave's friend Brian showed up. We are right in the thick of a discussion about the gospel at this point, and Brian leans in to listen to the conversation. Dave pauses, and he turns to his friend Brian. "So, man. What do you think about this?" After pontificating a bit, Brian asks me what I think about a related question: "What about the Muslims? I mean, they're serious too. They are willing to die for what they believe. Are you saying that they won't go to heaven?"

That's a lot to talk about! How would you respond? Dave is a genuine seeker who has questions about Hinduism and the reliability of the Gospels. Brian is asking me to defend Islam and explain why Muslims should or should not go to heaven. For all I know, Brian is a Muslim, or he might have close Muslim family or friends. I don't want to offend either of these guys, yet I also want to be true to the gospel. I don't want to hide the truth, but I also want to be sensitive and respectful of what they believe.[2]

Perhaps you've faced a similar dilemma. When others express their views or have direct questions about Christianity, how should we respond? Should we speak up and defend our faith? Do we insist on the

"What about the Muslims? They are willing to die for what they believe. Are you saying that they won't go to heaven?"

superiority of Christianity? Or do we avoid the conversation and let the questions go unanswered in loving tolerance of others' beliefs?

TOLERANCE: VIRTUE OR VICE?

Tolerance is often promoted as a virtue today, so the challenge to be respectful of the beliefs of others isn't an abstract issue. Speaking the truth about Christianity presents opportunity and pitfalls in our real, everyday relationships. In cities we are more likely to develop relationships with people from various religions. As we get to know them, we realize that people of other faiths can be kind and sincere. We may begin to realize that their character is the result of their religious belief, and it seems arrogant and disrespectful to insist that these beliefs are wrong. After all, by all appearances their religion has made them likable, respectable people.

Let's sharpen the dilemma even further. I have met secularists and Buddhists who are *more* generous and *more* sacrificial than many Christians I know. How should we respond to this, especially when non-Christians point it out to us? Does the fact that people of other religions can be moral, exhibiting kindness and respect that puts some Christians to shame, defeat our witness? Does it mean the gospel is not true?

If we don't settle these kinds of questions in advance, we will be unsure how to respond when they are asked. This isn't just an urban concern. Immigration patterns and globalized media make interaction with other religions a reality for all of us. In the town of Nacogdoches, in the Bible Belt of East Texas, my brother is discipling a Muslim. In fact, according to a report by the Carsey Institute, East Texas is one among many rural areas experiencing unprecedented levels of immigration.[3] With these new immigrants come new religious and spiritual beliefs.

Ubiquitous access to media has also dissolved several of the traditional urban versus rural boundaries. Regardless of our location, we are exposed to the same popular culture, the same news outlets, which often share common media biases. Often, the media promotes a policy of tolerance. For instance, the most acclaimed film of 2013, *Gravity*, drew viewers everywhere into a philosophical search for the meaning of life. Throughout the story, Buddha, Jesus, and humanism are presented as equally valid options. As Christians all over the country go to the movies, they are confronted with a question: Will you be tolerant and accepting, or will you be intolerant and exclusive?

So is religious tolerance a virtue or a vice? Those who see tolerance as a vice are quick to engage or condemn other faiths. They insist on the exclusive claims of Jesus and often dismiss the positive insights of other religions. But is it possible to see tolerance as a virtue as well? People who see tolerance as a virtue are often slow to share their faith out of respect for others' views. They don't talk about the exclusive claims of Jesus because they don't want to exclude others or hurt them. Out of love, they prefer not to demean others' beliefs. They believe it is wrong to enforce our beliefs on others. If you hold tolerance as a virtue, you tend to believe that everyone deserves the right to believe what he or she believes. So is it virtuous or traitorous to tolerate other religious and spiritual beliefs?

CLASSICAL TOLERANCE

In *The Intolerance of Tolerance*, D. A. Carson argues there are really two types of tolerance, the old and the new.[4] Old or "classical" tolerance holds the belief that *other opinions have a right to exist*. This type of tolerance allows for a diversity of viewpoints to flourish united around the common good. America was founded on this kind of tolerance, allowing for the freedom of religion. The political aim of this tolerance was the social good. Carson refers to this as social tolerance, where "people of different religions should mix together without slights and condescension."[5] This kind of tolerance, he says, is distinctly Christian.

Old tolerance is far older than America however. Some point to the Roman Empire as a paragon of tolerance. Oxford scholar Michael Green comments: "Roman religious policy in the early Empire was remarkably tolerant."[6] In the first century, Roman imperial policy allowed diverse

Classical tolerance holds the belief that *other opinions have a right to exist.*

religions to operate freely within the empire. Religions could add their gods to the Greco-Roman pantheon of gods or simply identify it with an existing deity.

But classical tolerance didn't begin with Rome. It goes back at least to the Persian Empire. Commenting on their policy of tolerance, Jon Berquist writes: "The empire did not try to enforce a single imperial language, culture, legal system, or religion ... [it] desired order — not necessarily a particular Persian way of life ... [it] seemed to promote a degree of acceptance and tolerance, even of pluralism, within all of its provinces."[7] In the Old Testament, King Cyrus permitted Israel to worship Yahweh freely and even financed the reconstruction of the Jewish temple. Cyrus's tolerance did Israel good. Persia acted as a providential imperium to ensure the survival of Israel and the Messiah's line.[8] In turn, Israel sought the good of the Persians. This mutual tolerance led to the flourishing of both Israel and Persia, leading to the preservation of the Jews and the thriving of the Persians.

We should also keep in mind the tolerance of God. Consider how God has been tolerant throughout history, permitting a wide array of beliefs, deities, and religious practices. Occasionally, he steps into history, bringing temporal judgment on other religions, but often he allows them to flourish, even though they are opposed to him.

How did Jesus respond to other religions? When we reflect on the Gospels, it is curious that Jesus never launched into tirades against the Romans, nor did he engage in lengthy diatribes denouncing the Greeks. When challenged by the Pharisees regarding the Roman imperial cult, he avoided slamming Caesar. His well-known remark, "Render

The cross is the height of classical tolerance, though it is certainly much more. God chose to roll back judgment day into the middle of history, onto his Son, so that idolaters of every stripe might be redeemed and accepted.

to Caesar the things that are Caesar's, and to God the things that are God's" (Matthew 22:21), was a clever way of maintaining classical tolerance. Honor the government, he said, unless it requires explicit dishonoring of God. Taxes can be paid to the temple *and* to the Roman Empire.

Jesus espoused the royal law: "Love your neighbor as yourself." His exemplary love compelled him to tolerate other beliefs, fraternize with Roman centurions, lay down the sword and pick up an ear, and love his enemies. In fact, one could argue that the cross is the height of classical tolerance, though it is certainly much more than that. Consider the delay of Christ's return. God chose to roll back the judgment day into the middle of history, onto his Son, so that self-absorbed people from every nation might hear the good news and be delivered.

In light of the patience God shows to those who do not deserve it, we should also be willing to respect and tolerate the beliefs of others. Contrary to the practice of the bigoted, intolerant "Christians" of Westboro Baptist Church in Kansas (who run a website called www.God-HatesIslam.com), we ought to grant others the right to believe whatever they desire to believe. What people believe is a deeply personal, profound matter. Settling on a religious belief isn't like picking out a ripe banana at the supermarket. Our beliefs require much more thought and investment. They represent commitments, decisions, and choices that define our identity. Loving our neighbor, then, entails valuing them and their beliefs. It respects the things they hold dear. As Christians love their neighbors and even their enemies, they should practice classical tolerance, winsomely granting people the right to hold beliefs different from their own. In this way, tolerance can be loving and respectful.

But how far should we go? How tolerant is too tolerant? After all, even the Romans had their limits. Despite their generous policy of religious tolerance, they required everyone to participate in worship of the "divine" Caesar. This, of course, is where the early Christians dug their heels in. And they paid the price. In AD 64 Nero lit his gardens with burning Christian bodies. Yes, tolerance has its limits.

THE NEW TOLERANCE

Tolerance *can* be an expression of Christian love, but it can also be an expression of relational and intellectual carelessness. How do you know if your tolerance is loving or careless? The answer depends on what kind of tolerance you are practicing. Where the old tolerance held that other opinions have a right to exist, the new tolerance is *the belief that all opinions are equally valid or true.* This is quite a leap away from the old tolerance. It is one thing to say something has the right to exist; it is altogether different to say that two beliefs are equally true. If we follow the logic of the new tolerance, it leads to inescapable contradictions. For example, you would end up affirming the following two statements:

> We should grant others the dignity to believe whatever they want.
> We should force others to believe whatever we believe to be true.

The new tolerance says that both of these beliefs are equally valid. But how can that be? We cannot simultaneously confer dignity on

The new tolerance is *the belief that all opinions are equally valid or true.*

opposing beliefs while also forcing people to give up those beliefs. The new tolerance is intellectually careless. It defies careful logic. And if we aren't aware of this important distinction between old and new tolerance, we can easily find ourselves boxed into a corner when we have conversations with others about our beliefs. We may genuinely want to respect others' views, yet easily mix up that desire by affirming what they believe to be equally true.

IS JESUS THE ONLY WAY?

Let's get specific and look at a concrete example. Consider this important question: "Is Jesus the only way to God?" Is there a way to talk about what you believe as a Christian, yet remain respectful of the beliefs of others? How do we navigate pluralism with the exclusive claims to the gospel?

Evangelical Christians believe that Jesus is the only way to God. The Christian faith teaches that Jesus is the only means to reconciling our broken relationship with God. Secularists and spiritually minded people find this difficult to believe. They insist no one can have an exclusive claim to God or to religious truth. There are many ways to God. This view is popularly called *religious pluralism.*[9]

Harvard University conducted research into religious pluralism and used Austin as a case-study city for the study called the Pluralism Project. I understand why they chose Austin. I regularly talk with committed pluralists. As I have reflected on these conversations, I've discovered at least three reasons why people embrace religious pluralism. They find religious pluralism to be more *enlightened,* more *humble,* and more *tolerant.* Let's explore each of these in more detail.

Is Religious Pluralism More Enlightened?

Some people consider the belief that all religious paths lead to the same God to be more *enlightened*. By this, they typically mean that it is an educated, thoughtful way to think about religious differences. Rather than choosing one religion or elevating one belief over others, you affirm them all. This sounds very accepting and progressive.

There is a problem with this approach, however. Basic familiarity with major world religions reveals that each religion teaches different things about who God is and how humans reach the divine. In fact, there are plenty of disagreements between the various religions regarding the *nature of God*. Buddhism, for example, doesn't believe in a personal God. Islam teaches something akin to an impersonal (nonrelational) monotheism. The Koran states that God reveals his will to us, but not his person. Christianity, however, teaches personal trinitarianism, that God exists as three persons in relationship, Father-Son-Spirit, who can be known and enjoyed. Hinduism holds various positions on the nature of God, ranging from polytheism to atheism. This is due to the absence of definitive revelation, such as the Koran or the Bible, that would clarify Hindu "theology." Instead, Hinduism has multiple sources of revelation (Upanishads, Vedas).[10] So, contrary to Islam, Hinduism has no presuppositions about the nature of God.

In short, the different major world religions differ extensively on their views of who or what God is. A respectful study of the major world religions suggests that it is far from "enlightened" to claim that all religions lead to the same God, when their views of God are, in fact, radically different. Any claim of religious pluralism contradicts the tenets of the religions themselves. This is far from accepting. Commenting on the inherent contradictions in today's religious pluralism, Boston College religion professor Stephen Prothero writes: "And it is comforting to pretend that the great religions make up one big, happy family. But this sentiment, however well-intentioned, is neither accurate nor ethically responsible. God is not one."[11]

Let's consider what different religions teach about *reaching the divine*. Buddhism suggests the Eightfold Noble Path, Islam has the Five

Pillars (Shahadah, Prayer, Fasting, Charity, Pilgrimage), and Christianity proclaims the gospel of Jesus. These share some surface level similarities, but are fundamentally different from one another. Prothero goes on to point out that religions are distinct and make different claims about God and how to reach him. Saying that all religions lead to God is not only unenlightened, it is plainly false. The new tolerance doesn't hold up to reality.

Is Religious Pluralism More Humble?

Despite the clear differences among the various world religions regarding the nature of God and human access to the divine, religious pluralists continue to insist that there are many ways to God. Why would an educated person persist in holding an inaccurate view of other religions? Another major reason is because they believe it is the most humble approach to take. I often hear people say: "Who am I to judge someone else's religion, to tell them that they are wrong?" This implies, of course, that maintaining particular beliefs about Jesus that are contrary to other religions is arrogant.

Now I'll be the first to admit there are plenty of arrogant Christians who rudely insist that Jesus is the only way to God. I apologize for them. I've been one myself. Arrogance, even about things that are true, runs counter to the life and teachings of Jesus, who was the model of humility. At the same time, we need to recognize that just because someone is arrogant about his or her beliefs doesn't make them wrong. People can be arrogant about all kinds of things — math, science, religion. You may know or work with someone who is arrogant, thinking they are always right and others are always wrong. The arrogant person likes to talk down to others with an air of superiority because they have the right answer. For Christians, this is unacceptable, a character issue that needs correction. Nevertheless, just because someone isn't nice about their beliefs doesn't mean they are incorrect. The question of truth is separate from the tone of its delivery.

Despite the many Christians who arrogantly despise other religious perspectives, there are others who have ardently studied the various world religions, compared their claims, and humbly came to the conclusion that Jesus was telling the truth, that personal faith in the Messiah is the only way to God. This doesn't make them arrogant; it makes them authentic. These individuals are willing to stand by what they have found to be true. They are men and women of conviction. Insisting that something is true doesn't automatically make one proud. After all, the exclusive truth claims of Christianity were originally made by Jesus himself, and Jesus was quintessentially humble. If his self-proclaimed message is taken at face value, it is hard to accuse him of hubris. He laid down his life for his enemies, to save those who rejected and despised him.

When religious pluralism claims that there are many ways to God, it is not being humble. The tolerance of religious pluralism actually carries an air of arrogance with it. How? Consider that religious pluralism *insists* that *its* view—that all ways lead to God—is true while all other religions are false in their teachings. Religious pluralism is dogmatic in its insistence on its own exclusive claim that all roads lead to God. It holds to this even when this claim directly contradicts the deeply held convictions of those who practice Islam, Hinduism, Judaism, and Christianity. The claim of the religious pluralist is arrogant because it seeks to enforce its own belief on others. It says to those who humbly and faithfully practice other religions: "You must believe what I believe, not what you believe. Your way isn't right; in fact all of your ways are wrong and my way is right. There isn't just one way to God (insert your religion); there are many ways. You are wrong and I am right."

In some cases, the person saying this hasn't really studied what the various world religions teach in any depth, yet they make this blind assertion. Where is the proof that this is true? To what ancient Scriptures, traditions, and careful reasoning can they point? The lack of historical and rational support for religious pluralism makes it highly untenable. Saying that all paths lead to God is not more humble.

Is Religious Pluralism Truly Tolerant?

The final objection you might hear is that religious pluralism is more tolerant than Christianity. As we've seen, tolerance, in the classical sense, simply

The claim of the religious pluralist is arrogant because it seeks to enforce its own belief on others. It says to those who humbly and faithfully practice other religions: "You must believe what I believe, not what you believe. Your way isn't right; in fact all of your ways are wrong and my way is right. There isn't just one way to God (insert your religion); there are many ways. You are wrong and I am right."

means that other beliefs and religious perspectives have a right to exist. I'll be the first to say that we need more of this kind of tolerance. Christians should be accommodating of other beliefs, giving everyone the dignity to believe what they want without forcing their beliefs on others. But does religious pluralism allow for this? Often, it does not. Instead of accommodating spiritual differences and respecting them and those who hold to them, religious pluralism tries to blunt them and minimize the differences.

The claim that all paths lead to the same God is the assertion of a new religious claim. When someone tells you that you need to be more tolerant because all paths lead to the same God, they are making a truth claim. This claim blunts distinctions between religions, throwing them all in one pot and mixing them together, saying, "They all get us to God, so the differences don't really matter!" But this isn't tolerance; it's a power play. The distinctive and different views of God and how to reach the divine in Buddhism, Hinduism, Christianity, and Islam are brushed aside in a single, powerful swoop. The Eightfold Noble Path, the Five Pillars of Islam, and the gospel of Christ are not tolerated (respected for what they are); instead, they are forced to submit to a new religious claim. Religious pluralism might *appear* tolerant, but in reality it is placing itself above other religions, in a position of power. It assumes power and authority, making determinations of truth that are contrary to other religions.

PERSUASIVE TOLERANCE: RESPONDING TO PLURALISM

People spend years studying and practicing their particular religions. Telling those who have religious convictions that they don't really matter is the height of arrogance and intolerance. The idea of religious tolerance assumes there are differences to tolerate, but pluralism is intolerant of those differences. In this sense, *religious pluralism is a religion of its own.* It has its own religious absolute — all paths lead to the same God — and requires people of other faiths to embrace this absolute. Those who argue for religious pluralism by saying it is more enlightened, humble, or tolerant are actually engaging in evangelism for their pluralistic beliefs. Religious pluralism is preachy, but under the guise of tolerance. Again, writer Stephen Prothero points this out: "Faith in the unity of religions is just that—faith (perhaps even a kind of fundamentalism). And the leap that gets us there is an act of the hyperactive imagination."[12] Its faith to believe in religious pluralism— that there are many paths that all lead to God—is not an observable, self-evident fact; it requires a leap of faith.

As we have seen, each of the reasons for subscribing to religious pluralism—enlightenment, humility, and tolerance—all backfire. They don't carry through. Religious pluralism isn't enlightened, it's inaccurate; it isn't humble, it's fiercely dogmatic; and it isn't really all that tolerant because it intolerantly blunts religious distinctions. In the end, religious pluralism is a religion itself. It is a religion based on contradictions.

True Christianity, by contrast, has a history of respecting and honoring the beliefs of other religions. Christianity engages these beliefs by drawing comparisons and highlighting similarities and differences, honoring the unique principles of Karma (Hinduism), Enlightenment (Buddhism), Submission (Islam), and Grace (Christianity).

What, then, is an appropriate Christian response to other religious beliefs?

Christ Teaches Us Humility

Again, let's consider Jesus' approach. Jesus exclusively claimed to be the way, the truth, and the life (John 14:6). What does this mean? Does it mean that Jesus is our trailblazer, clearing the other religious options aside so we can hike our way to heaven through spiritual or moral improvement? If we keep the Ten Commandments, if we serve the poor and love our neighbor, if we pray and read the Bible enough, then perhaps God will accept us? Not quite. As *the way*, Jesus doesn't create a path for us to hike. The gospel begins with the bad news that we can never make it—we can never do enough spiritual, moral, or social good to impress God. We can't make it up the path. We all fail to love and serve the infinitely admirable and lovable God. In fact, if we love other things more, that's a crime of infinite proportions. It's against an infinite God. The sentence for our crime must be carried out. That's the bad news, but it is the bad news that makes the good news good.

Jesus doesn't clear a path for us to follow; instead, he takes the arduous hike for us, going down into the valley of the shadow of death where the criminals die. He hikes down into our sin, our rebellion, and our failures. He heaps them all on his back and climbs on a cross, where he is punished for our crime, a bloody gruesome death. The innocent man is punished for the guilty. If he doesn't take our punishment, then we must endure it — forever separated from God.

Rejecting Jesus has infinite consequences. But for those who embrace Jesus in his sin-absorbing death, there is forgiveness. Jesus hikes, not only through the valley, but up the mountain to the Father, where he pleads our innocence (see Hebrews 7:25; 10:1 – 18). This is what it means for Jesus to be the way. He is the redemptive way to a restored relationship with God. He deals justly with our crimes by taking our place as our substitute. Seeing this should make us incredibly *humble* and not arrogant. The gospel reveals how undeserving we are, and it shows us just how much mercy we have been given.

Christ Enlightens Us

Jesus is also *the truth*. What does that mean? In John 1, we are told that God became flesh and was full of grace and truth in Jesus. *The truth is that God is Jesus.* Christianity is the only religion where God is born as a man, fully human in every sense of the word. All other religions teach that human beings must work their way toward divinity. But the truth is Jesus. The truth is not found in our attempts to climb the spiritual ladder to God, to experience a vision of the divine. It is God coming down to us, becoming one of us, dying in our place, for our crimes. God comes to us, resurrecting us in our spiritual death and giving us his life. God works his way down to humanity — that's grace. Truth isn't a special prayer or a code word we say at the pearly gates. In Christianity, the truth is revealed in a person, Jesus, who is full of grace and truth. Other religions teach that God is impersonal, distant, inaccessible, or beyond relating to. But in Christianity we meet God in the flesh. The truth is known as a Person who dies and rises for us.

Persuasive Tolerance

Finally, Jesus is *the life*. In John's gospel, Jesus says that he is the resurrection and the life, that whoever believes in him, though they die, yet they will live (John 11:25). He descends into the valley to take our death, rising up from the dead and ascending to prepare a new place for us to enjoy life with him forever. In the end, it doesn't matter how nice or moral a person is because there is not enough niceness or morality to pay for our rejection of God. Either we are rejected, or we turn to Jesus who was rejected for us. This is the heart of the gospel. Jesus lays down his life for those who reject him, for his enemies, for those who don't believe in him, and he offers them forgiveness.

This means that our lives are not our own to do with as we please. If Jesus is our life, we belong to him. As the apostle Paul once said: "I have been crucified with Christ. It is no longer I who live, but Christ who lives in me. And the life I now live in the flesh I live by faith in the Son of God, who loved me and gave himself for me" (Galatians 2:19–20). Since we belong to another, we aren't out to prove ourselves right, to seek power over others, or to force other people to believe what we believe. We know that salvation is a gift of grace. Instead of being arrogant, we are humbled by God's grace.

Faith in Jesus should lead us into *persuasive tolerance*. Persuasive tolerance starts with deep convictions, but without the motive of forcing or manipulating others to agree with us. We enter into dialogue with other faiths out of a genuine desire to learn and to share what we believe. We do not abandon our deeply held convictions. That would be inauthentic. Instead, persuasive tolerance extends people the dignity of their own beliefs, while also freely making a case for one's own belief. It does not minimize the differences between religions, but honors them. Jesus is our way, he is our truth, he is our life. And this produces humility and true enlightenment as we come to experience the grace of God and grasp that God has come down to us, dying for our moral and religious failures, and has offered us new life.

Persuasive tolerance starts with deep convictions, but without the motive of forcing or manipulating others to agree with us. We enter into dialogue with other faiths out of a genuine desire to learn and to share what we believe. We do not abandon our deeply held convictions. That would be inauthentic. Instead, persuasive tolerance extends people the dignity of their own beliefs, while also freely making a case for one's own belief.

If we believe that eternal life is only found in knowing Jesus Christ, then tolerant persuasion is an act of love.

If this is true, the appropriate response is to lovingly try to persuade others to believe in Jesus—who alone offers the wonderful promise of forgiveness. As World Vision International director of interfaith relations Chawkat Moucarry says: "It is perfectly legitimate for believers who take seriously the exclusive claims of their religion to try to persuade others of the truth they proclaim. There is nothing wrong with hoping and even expecting that some people, having carefully examined these claims, will make a life-changing decision as a result of transparent and free dialogue."[13] Recall the words of atheist Penn Jilette, "How much do you have to hate somebody to believe everlasting life is possible and not tell them?"[14] If we believe that eternal life is only found in knowing Jesus Christ, then tolerant persuasion is an act of love.

Every person has a choice they must make—where will we place our faith? Will we place it in a dogmatic and intolerant pluralism? Or will we place it in Jesus, whose way is humble, whose truth is enlightening, and whose life demonstrates persuasive tolerance of others by respecting their choices and decisions?

Both Christianity and pluralism require faith. In *The Gospel in a Pluralist Society*, Lesslie Newbigin writes: "Doubt is not autonomous."[15] In other words, you can't rely on doubt alone, doubting that anything and everything is true. You can't doubt one thing without placing your faith in another. You can doubt Jesus and trust pluralism, or you can trust Jesus and doubt pluralism. But you cannot say, "I believe Jesus is the only way," and also say, "I believe all religions lead to God."

The "new" tolerance is on the rise. It is popular, often thrown out in discussions without much thought. As we have seen, however, it is intellectually careless, exclusive, and intolerant. It exclusively claims that its policy of self-contradictory tolerance is the only religious view that works. It denies the distinctive views of other religions and makes the exclusive claim that all religions lead to the same God. It dismisses the centuries of study, formulation, adherence, and practice of religious devotees. It makes an exclusive claim (all beliefs are equally true) and intolerantly forces that belief onto everyone.

There is quite a difference between the old tolerance and the new. Granting others the dignity of their beliefs means that we acknowledge the real differences between religious views. We promote respectful dialogue and charitable debate between religions. Christians should honor other worldviews and be willing to dialogue with people of other faiths to better understand their own distinctive beliefs.[16] We should be eager to learn from others, not fearful or condemning of them. Meaningful conversation is in short supply, and of all people, Christians should be having meaningful conversations about these matters with others. After all, Jesus claimed that he alone had the answers to the deepest questions of life. If we believe his teachings are true, we have every reason to talk deeply with others about the life, message, and teaching of Jesus. Jesus gives us every reason to be classically tolerant, full of love, and persuasively engaged in the things that matter most.

KEY QUESTIONS

1. Share a time that you encountered someone with a different faith. How did you respond?
2. What's the difference between old and new tolerance? Which do you tend toward?
3. What frees us to allow people the dignity of their own beliefs?
4. How should Christians respond to the claims of pluralism?
5. What would persuasive tolerance look like in your existing relationships?

chapter five

UNINFORMED WITNESS: THINKING SECURELY

One of the most common objections I hear when I talk to people about evangelism is: "I don't know enough." People say, "What if someone asks me a question I don't have an answer to?" They are reluctant to talk about Christ because they are concerned they won't know how to respond when someone asks, "How can Jesus be the only way to God?" or "Doesn't the Bible have lots of errors?"

These are serious questions that deserve thoughtful responses.[1] As Christians, we should have *reasons* for our hope, for the things we believe are true.[2] If we hope without adequate reason, then what good is our faith? If it can't stand up to the test of good questions and hard times, is it worth banking on? Having knowledge about what you claim to believe is important, both for your own faith and for your witness to others. So how much do we need to know before we are ready to witness confidently to the resurrected Christ? What if we don't know enough? How do we defeat this defeater?

THINKING CHRISTIANITY

Have you ever had an experience when your beliefs were challenged and you had no answers? Maybe you ended up sheepishly walking away from a conversation. When I was in graduate school, I worked as a night guard for a creative advertising firm. While I didn't wear a cop outfit, I did carry around a black, five-pound Maglite and a small flip phone for emergencies. The firm was housed in an old, renovated, five-story convent, tucked away on a hill in the middle of a forest. Think Bruce Wayne's manor—stunning by day, creepy by night.

Night after night the cleaning crew would come in to work, and I got to know Tony, the owner of the cleaning business, quite well. Tony was an ox of a man, girded with intellectual strength and classic, Italian tenacity. He was an armchair philosopher—and a principled agnostic. At the time, I was a theology student, eager to talk about my faith in Jesus. And man, did we talk! I grew to admire Tony's intellectual integrity, his openness to reason and dialogue, and after several conversations we developed a friendship. Often I found myself walking away from our conversations with more questions than answers. Toward the end of one conversation, he dismissed C. S. Lewis's *Mere Christianity* as a shallow defense of Christianity, one that didn't address his questions. That caught me off guard! Because of Tony's constant questions, I was forced to develop reasonable explanations for my beliefs.

Many today consider Christianity to be an unthinking faith, something for the mindless masses. But the Bible underscores the importance of reason, frequently calling us to think and to engage our minds:

- And you shall love the Lord your God with all your heart and with all your soul and *with all your mind* and with all your strength. (Mark 12:30)
- So he *reasoned* in the synagogue with the Jews and the devout persons, and in the marketplace every day with those who happened to be there. (Acts 17:17; cf. 17:2; 18:4, 19)
- By faith we *understand* that the universe was created by the word of God. (Hebrews 11:3)
- Have no fear of them, nor be troubled, but in your hearts honor Christ the Lord as holy, *always being prepared to make a defense to anyone who asks you for a reason* for the hope that is in you. (1 Peter 3:14–15, italics added in all cases)

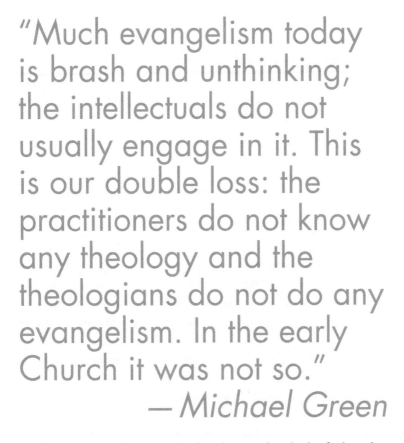

"Much evangelism today is brash and unthinking; the intellectuals do not usually engage in it. This is our double loss: the practitioners do not know any theology and the theologians do not do any evangelism. In the early Church it was not so."
— *Michael Green*

These are just a few examples, but there are hundreds of others that show the necessity of having a "thinking" Christianity. Taken together, these texts teach us that the active engagement of our minds is necessary for worship, preaching, apologetics, and faith. Peter admonishes us to have reasons for our beliefs. The phrase he uses means "to make a defense," and it comes from the Greek word *apologia*, from which we get the word "apologetics." An apologetic isn't a defensive, antagonistic argument. It is a reasoned statement of gospel belief, often presented in response to questions about the Christian faith. It requires us to address questions, objections, and concerns using cultural idioms, speaking in a way that people can understand.

In fact, in *Evangelism in the Early Church*, Michael Green highlights five characteristics that led the early Christians to infectiously spread the gospel throughout a hostile Roman Empire. One of these characteristics was a commitment to *apologetics*. Unfortunately such thoughtful evangelism is not common today: "Much evangelism today is brash and unthinking; the intellectuals do not usually engage in it. This is our double loss: the practitioners do not know any theology and the theologians do not do any evangelism. In the early Church it was not so."[3] We would do well to follow the example of Jonathan Edwards, of whom it was said: "All his theology was practical, and all his practice was logical."

In Acts 22, Paul makes a defense for the gospel against his Jewish persecutors. His defense is a unique mix. He highlights his credentials, shares some selective stories, and engages with Jewish theology. At another time, when Paul was speaking with the Athenians in Acts 17:22–31, he took a different approach. He "thought out" and defended the gospel by engaging with Hellenistic philosophy and poetry, a conversational approach. Thinking faith isn't a matter of rehearsing canned apologetic defenses; it's a commitment to thinking deeply about the implications of the gospel in various cultures and then working to communicate that to people in those contexts.

As we see in Paul's life, there is room to learn as you go. Paul freely drew on things he saw and experienced as he traveled and interacted with people in different cities. Cultural claims form good fodder for evangelism. In fact, they often touch on or reflect gospel truths that we can connect with. In Athens, Paul saw an idol to an unknown god and used it as an example. He cited lyrics from the culture. This probably was not a part of his formal theological training with Rabbi Gamaliel. A thinking faith requires a willingness to learn and to adapt to circumstances so that we can communicate the gospel fluently in ideas, idioms, and words our hearers can understand.

This means that you will have times, like I did, when you head home with more questions than answers. That's okay! That's far better than responding in frustration or arrogance, holding to a "blind," anti-intellectual Christianity. Remember Peter's admonition to have a ready explanation for our hope, something that God gives to each of us. Thinking Christianity isn't just for the Peters and Pauls—it's for all of us! Paul tells those everyday Colossians: "Walk in wisdom toward outsiders, making the best use of the time. Let your speech always be gracious, seasoned with salt, so that you may know how you ought to answer each person" (Colossians 4:5–6). This evangelistic admonition reminds us that gospel communication is an ordinary affair. Walk in wisdom, speak with grace, and know how to answer *each* person you meet. These actions aren't something you prepare for with memorized responses; rather, they are the fruit of an engaged and responsive

Thinking faith isn't a matter of rehearsing canned apologetic defenses; it's a commitment to thinking deeply about the implications of the gospel in various cultures and then working to communicate that to people in those contexts.

Christianity. They are the result of regular times of reflection, personal encounters with God, and the practice of conversing with others.

GETTING BEYOND INSECURITY

Even if you are intimidated by words like evangelism and apologetics, I hope you can see the value in cultivating a thinking faith, one that is eager to learn how to communicate the gospel wisely with others. Remember that engaging in apologetics doesn't mean being defensive or having an argument locked and loaded. It can be a simple, clear, and reasoned statement of the gospel in cultural idiom, something that addresses your listener's actual life, especially his objections and concerns. The alternative to thinking about your faith is rehearsing information or going through a presentation that doesn't ring true with people. They will find it literally unbelievable. No one likes being a spiritual project. People want to be known. Being inefficient with our time and generous with our interest will enable us to listen to their questions and get to thoughtful and personal answers.

Still, I understand that speaking up can be intimidating. It's especially true when we don't have control over how people will respond. What if we don't know how to communicate the gospel in a way that makes sense to the person we are talking with? How do we face the fear of not knowing what to say? When these fears arise, we need something to give us security. So how do we overcome our fears, building up the confidence to speak, particularly when we are afraid we don't have the right answers? What frees us to be able to offer discerning explanations for our faith?

There are two kinds of security that can free us to engage in apologetics. The first is *intellectual security*. The Christian faith has a long tradition of apologists who have faithfully defended the faith for centuries, often answering some of the same questions for different times and cultures. Some of the earliest apologists include Justin Martyr, Tertullian, Tatian, and Clement of Alexandria. Their apologetic answers have continued to be handed down from generation to generation. Today, newer apologists such as Ravi Zacharias, William Lane Craig, Tim Keller, John Frame, and Alvin Plantinga address old and new questions.[4] We do well to read them.

In addition to answering specific questions, there is value in growing in our knowledge and understanding of the gospel itself. The gospel acts as a grand apologetic by addressing the deepest of life's questions: the value of creation, the problem of evil and suffering, the existence of God, the hope of salvation, the nature of God and man, and the role of faith. The story line of the Bible is an explanatory narrative that accounts for our deepest longings and hopes, while narrating a world we all want.[5] It begins and ends with a perfect world—just, joyful, beautiful, intimate, fruitful, creative, and full of peace. The story of

The gospel is a word about an event that changed the course of history in the person of Jesus. This word makes sense of a world where things are not as they are supposed to be, and it offers deep, truthful answers to some of life's hardest questions.

Scripture also acknowledges most of our objections to the way the world currently is—unjust, sad, lonely, cursed, barren, and broken.

Underneath these true descriptions, the Bible goes further, identifying the problem—the world order, the sinful longings of "the flesh," and the devil himself—as well as providing the solution—the life, death, resurrection, and return of Jesus Christ our Lord. Apologetics enable the gospel story—the bad news of our sin and its consequences and the good news of God's redemption and rescue—to be heard. It reveals the inner coherence of Christianity and its intellectual credibility, and it offers an existentially satisfying purpose for anyone who will trust in Christ. The gospel is a word about an event that changed the course of history in the person of Jesus. This word makes sense of a world where things are not as they are supposed to be, and it offers deep, truthful answers to some of life's hardest questions. Although the worldview presented in the Bible does furnish us with intellectual security, it is often not enough to embolden our witness. We need something more.

DEEP SECURITY

There is another type of security that goes beyond our understanding and our intellect, freeing us to offer reasonable explanations for our faith. Let's return once more to Peter's words, which are often quoted out of context. Prior to charging us to have a ready defense of our faith, he exhorts us to "*have no fear of them, nor be troubled, but in your hearts honor Christ the Lord as holy,* always being prepared to make a defense to anyone who asks you for a reason for the hope that is in you" (1 Peter 3:14–15, italics added). What could be deeper than a reasonable hope expressed through a biblical worldview?[6] How might Peter have in mind something besides a clear, rational defense of the faith? While 1 Peter 3:14 is a hallmark text for many apologetic ministries, verse 14 actually addresses the heart, not the head: "In your *hearts* honor Christ the Lord as holy." Peter was writing to fearful people who were afraid of persecution. Although the threat of physical persecution is rare in the West, we do face alternate forms of persecution today.

The persecution the Western church faces today is more subtle and clandestine than the physical persecutions of the first century. Cultural apologist at Mars Hill Audio, Ken Myers, agrees: "The challenge of living with popular culture may well be as serious for modern Christians as persecution and plagues were for the saints of earlier centuries."[7] Whether Christians are facing life-threatening persecution or oppressive ideology of popular, pluralistic culture, we all share a common foe—heartfelt fear. When we struggle to share our faith today, we face some of the same basic fears of rejection and ridicule. When we engage in conversation with a skeptic, we encounter feelings of inadequacy. We are overpowered by an encroaching enemy, who attacks our thoughts to undermine our confidence, diminishes our trust in Christ, and redirects us away from speaking about Jesus. The "Defeater" whispers: "You won't have all the right answers. Do you really think you can convince this person to trust Jesus? You should bring them a book instead or just let a smarter Christian talk to them." This is a cunning form of persecution.

"The challenge of living with popular culture may well be as serious for modern Christians as persecution and plagues were for the saints of earlier centuries."
— Ken Meyers

As we saw in the previous chapter, the pluralistic culture of twenty-first century America claims to be accepting of diverse religious views, yet claims that are exclusive, like the uniqueness of Jesus or the claims of Christian ethics, are often rejected. Our country is less Christian than it has ever been (though politics and media exaggerate this disaffection). The culture wars, many say, have been lost. We are inheriting the fallout of "bad religion,"[8] and some are even announcing the death of Christianity in America.[9] Media bias looms large, and behind these cultural trends exist spiritual powers (Ephesians 6:12; Colossians 2:15), forces that aim to intimidate, weaken, and destabilize the church. There is an all-out attack against Christian faith. Our enemy does not need to use visible demonic activity because his invisible deceptions are effective enough. The American church is in his crosshairs.

It can be difficult to answer objections and sympathize with skeptics when we feel inadequate. It's tough to sort through all the pop philosophy and bumper sticker truth claims. But Peter is correct; we need to have a reasonable defense for our faith. That's why we need to understand that a reasonable defense is not always "the right answer." To be sure, we must have clarity on the gospel and understand how it is good news for others, but must everyone become a professional apologist? I don't think so. *While we may not have the ability to answer every question, Jesus gives us the ability to be secure in our faith.*

Circling back to Peter's exhortation to the early church, he writes: "Have *no fear of them*, nor be troubled, but in your hearts honor Christ the Lord as holy" (1 Peter 3:14). He reassures early Christian believers facing mockery and hatred to sink their security deep into their hearts and not just their intellect. If we fear what people might ask or say, right answers won't be able to rescue us. Similarly, a persecuted Christian fearing for their life isn't rescued by fine apologetics. Our security breach is deeper than our intellectual shortcomings—it runs deep, into our hearts. There the enemy plays on our fears, chases us into the shadows, and lays a media-sized hand over our mouths. *True apologetics begins with heartfelt confidence in Jesus.*

In Christ, we possess a power that can rip the muzzle off, chase away the shadows, and bolster winsome, authentic gospel witness. That power lifted Jesus out of the grave, but it sits latent in our blanketed heart, where we are inordinately troubled by what others think. Beneath the blanket of persecution there often lies a golden idol, the one thing we cannot live without—the approval of others. We pine for the approval of others and would rather quiet down about the good news than speak up and risk our coworker thinking we are preachy, impersonal, or intolerant. Our reluctance to talk about Jesus springs from a desire to gain the approval of others instead of resting in the approval of God our Father. We desperately need to set apart Jesus as Lord *in our hearts*, not what others think as Lord. This is where *deep security* is found. To get there, the idol has to be replaced with a greater God who offers deeper security and meaning. We need the gift of repentance, regularly, to exchange our worship of what others think of us for what God the Father thinks of us in Christ—fully loved, full accepted, no condemnation, no rejection.

You have every resource, every truth, and every power available to you in Christ. You are more than a conqueror in Christ Jesus (Romans 8:37). The key is learning to remain in Christ. Let's look to the early church to see how they did this.

We desperately need to set apart Jesus as Lord *in our hearts*, not what others think as Lord. This is where *deep security* is found.

THE POWER OF THE GOSPEL

The bold witness of the Thessalonian Christians was famous in the first century. People around the world heard about their fear-conquering witness amidst persecution: "Not only has the word of the Lord sounded forth from you in Macedonia and Achaia, but your faith in God has gone forth everywhere" (1 Thessalonians 1:8). How did the Thessalonians do it? How did they snap their fear of human beings and testify of Jesus, amidst their sufferings? Paul tells us: "because our gospel came to you not only in word, but also in power and in the Holy Spirit and with full conviction" (1 Thessalonians 1:4–5). The gospel they believed and received wasn't just a theological construct or a churchy platitude. Sure, it came through spoken and written words, and it was preached, taught, and shared. But it also came in power.

Often Christians are either "word" people or "power" people. On the one hand, we may lean toward a rationalized Christianity. This type of Christianity holds to the gospel Word without gospel power. It preaches, teaches, catechizes, studies, memorizes, and shares the word but with little effect. It possesses "wise and persuasive words" but not "demonstration of the Spirit and of power" (1 Corinthians 2:4). This kind of Christianity can master systematic, biblical, and historical theology without being mastered by Christ. It can identify idols but remains powerless to address their power. Why? Because it replaces the power of the Spirit with the power of knowledge.

On the other hand, there is an equal danger in spiritualized Christianity. Such Christianity prays, sings, shouts, and claims victory over a lost world without lifting a finger to share God's gospel. It is not enough to pray for power; we must proclaim God's Word. The power of the Spirit works through the proclaimed Word. Faith comes by hearing, and hearing by the word of Christ. My pastor during college, Tom Nelson, always said: "Don't just stand on a shovel and pray for a hole." Spiritualized Christianity tends to stand and pray, emphasizing private or emotional experiences with God. What we need is prayer and proclamation, power and Word.

The Thessalonians had word *and* power, they grew in understanding and experience, but they also had *full conviction*. It is not enough to have spiritual power and good theology. These must also be coupled with *faith*, an active embrace of God's promises in Christ, which brings about conviction. Full conviction comes when we are set free from false forms of security and experience Spirit-empowered faith in the word of Christ. It springs from genuine encounter with Christ. Full conviction transcends intellectual doubt *and* emotional experiences, and in the silence of persecution it says: "Christ is enough." True security, deep security, comes through the reasonable, powerful, Christ-centered conviction that Jesus is enough, not only for us but for the world. When we falter, the church is present to exhort, encourage, and pray for one another to set apart Christ as Lord in our hearts. May we toss out the penny stocks of the fear of man to invest deeply in the limitless riches of Christ.

A believable gospel is a gospel in stereo—a reasonable explanation given with Spirit-filled power. Study, learn, and think. At the same time, give up your idols and learn to rest in Jesus, and the power of the Spirit will flow. As a result, you'll be more sensitive to his promptings and more confident in your calling. You won't mistake knowledge or experience as the barometer of faith. Instead, you'll combine word and power with faith, setting apart Jesus in your heart. When the enemy

Full conviction transcends intellectual doubt *and* emotional experiences, and in the silence of persecution says: "Christ is enough."

rises to tell you, "You don't know enough" or "You do know enough," recognize the persecuting power behind those words and cling to the word of Christ, who is more than enough. Christ is enough for you and he is enough for those who don't believe. Take heart; the gospel is "the power of God for salvation to everyone who believes" (Romans 1:16)—everyone!

KEY QUESTIONS

1. Have you ever met anyone like Tony? How did you respond to their superior knowledge? How would you change that now?
2. What do you think the next step is for you to engage in "thinking Christianity"?
3. What keeps you from deep security in Christ? What other "lords" do you look to for approval and satisfaction?
4. Why were the Thessalonians exemplary gospel witnesses?
5. Are power and word enough for bold witness? Why or why not?
6. How might the Spirit be calling you to respond to the Lord in prayer right now?

02 RE-EVANGELIZATION

This section is represented by a continuous circle to symbolize the ongoing need for Christians to experience renewal by addressing their evangelistic defeaters with the gospel. Its depth and circular motion remind us of the need to continually communicate the eternal gospel in new ways to various cultures and people.

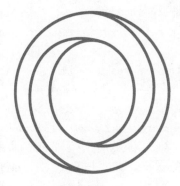

In the previous section, we examined four defeaters that, if heeded, can help us avoid unbelievable evangelism. My aim in reflecting on these defeaters has been to affirm and challenge these concerns in order to fill out a much bigger, more believable vision for evangelism. I hope those chapters have inspired you to be a more authentic, patient, and discerning evangelist. By now, you're probably ready to get on with the actual gospel metaphors. However, if we head straight into evangelistic methods, we could easily go astray again. To avoid running off track, we need *re-evangelization — a fresh preaching of the gospel to Christians and for cultures.*

The first front for re-evangelization is probably clear. We face an urgent need to learn how to communicate the gospel in secularized Western culture. This will require personal and cultural discernment in order to know how to communicate the gospel to others effectively. Not everyone needs to hear the same version of the gospel message. This is sometimes called the "missional" task.

The second front for re-evangelization hits closer to home — the church — and is an "ecclesial" task. Re-evangelization isn't just a matter of communicating in intelligible, culturally relevant ways. We can heed evangelism critiques and gain fresh witnessing methods, and remain unmotivated to share the gospel. Why? Because there is a defeater underneath the defeaters — *fear of what others think of us.* We can avoid all the evangelistic pitfalls and still refuse to speak about Christ because we are afraid that others will still think those things about us. Therefore, both evangelized Christians and insufficiently evangelized cultures need a fresh preaching of the gospel.

To do this, I recommend a *multisensory approach*, employing the senses of sight, touch, and sound, to reinvigorate gospel witness. Each sense is critical to whole understanding and diverse communication of the message of Jesus. As we have seen in the defeaters, a correct vision of the gospel is essential to handling the gospel properly. However, if we don't know some of the various gospel options, we will be limited in connecting Christ to different life contexts. Our goal is gospel fluency, cultivating skill in speaking the gospel into personal situations and cultural contexts. To this end, the next three chapters will:

1. *Clarify our sight* with a fresh vision of the gospel message.
2. *Diversify our ability to touch or handle* the gospel through different metaphors.
3. *Hone our speech to communicate* the gospel in cultural key.

This multisensory approach will immerse us in the inexhaustible riches of Christ, resulting in the re-evangelization of Christians who, in turn, are reinvigorated and equipped to re-evangelize cultures.

chapter six

CLARITY: GAINING A FRESH VISION OF THE GOSPEL

In Don DeLillo's prescient novel *White Noise*, Jack is a middle-class professor of Hitler Studies (a department he made up) at College-on-the-Hill. As a professor, he struggles with what others think of him. Many of his colleagues are fluent in German, but Jack can't read the language, much less speak it. He secretly enlists a private German tutor, but struggles to grasp the language. In a discussion about the plot to kill Hitler, Jack remarks: "All plots tend to move deathward." The inevitable conclusion of every story is death, both for the plotter and the plotted, and Jack is deathly afraid of it. Fear follows him around like a toxic airborne event. His internal dialogue is a persistent trial by jury of what others think. He is afraid of being found out, afraid of losing others, afraid of the truth. Are you ever afraid of being found out as a Christian? Or perhaps of losing your reputation in some way? One of the things that blurs our vision of the gospel most is an inordinate concern with how others see us.

Reputation means everything to us. A person of "good repute" is someone who has good character. Character is what comes out of people in a pinch. When you squeeze the tube, whatever is inside comes out. Good character or bad character. When the milk is spilt, the character is seen — patient or impatient. So, reputation is a reflection of innate character. It isn't something we finesse or manage; it just becomes visible over time. Character comes before reputation.

Unfortunately, we often flip that order. We've put reputation before character. We try to manage what people think about us without cultivating the character to work from. This is true across our culture where political parties and media spin news to reinforce an agenda. Companies pay inordinate sums to create brands, artists hire PR agents to foster a public persona, and individuals build platforms behind their computers through blogging and social media. In all of this "reputation building," we often care more about the opinions of others than in God's opinion of us. We are plagued by thoughts such as: "Do they see me as kind, thoughtful, tolerant, and knowledgeable, or as mean, ignorant, bigoted, and daft?" We do whatever is necessary to keep up our preferred reputation.

All of this seems perfectly acceptable in the business world. It's called impression management. It's okay to create a reputation that isn't there by "fluffing" your résumé or telling a few white lies to impress a client. But in the biblical world it's called double-mindedness and is fraught with instability (James 1:5 – 8). Double-minded people separate reputation from character, and their words become an exercise in impression management. It leads to doing and saying different things for different people. Instead of one Jonathan, over time several versions of yourself emerge in order to gain the approval of others — the tolerant Jonathan, the gospel-centered Jonathan, the neighborly Jonathan, the artsy Jonathan, the sports enthusiast Jonathan (now I'm definitely lying!). We get caught up in a game of perception. This idolatry of reputation becomes so strong that we can't imagine our versions being shattered. That would be a kind of death, a blow to our socially constructed source of self-worth.

Jack continues to converse with his wife about death as things hit a climax. It turns out that she too is afraid of death, so afraid that she has been taking an experimental drug especially designed to fight off fear. Jack reflects:

How strange it is. We have these deep terrible lingering fears about ourselves and the people we love. Yet we walk around, talk to people, eat and drink. We manage to function. The feelings are deep and real. Shouldn't they paralyze us? . . . How is it no one sees how deeply afraid we were, last night, this morning? Is it something we all hide from each other, by mutual consent? Or do we share the same secret without knowing it? Wear the same disguise?[1]

It is time we got our secret out in the light. Whether by mutual consent or by ignorance, we all walk around wearing the same disguise. Can we agree to rip it off in repentance, to escape the shadows and return to the light? Until we do, fear of death by loss of reputation will silence the good news. We will remain paralyzed, unevangelized and unevangelizing, scared to death. We will not risk our "reputation" for fear of losing favor with others. We won't speak up about the God-intoxicating time of worship on Sunday, the deep time of community on Wednesday, or the joy of Christ every day because we don't want people to think we are weird, narrow-minded, or religious. If people found out, we might even be a little embarrassed.

Spellbound by the approval of others and ensnared by fear of embarrassment, we hold our beliefs close and our Savior distant. Burk Parsons comments: "It may very well be the case that embarrassment is the most feared form of persecution for many Christians today."[2] This persecution is real. We need liberation. We need hope, and like any persecution, our only hope is Christ. Recanting the faith in fear will not preserve our lives but destroy them. We will die with a Christless reputation. The way out is through the liberating power of repentance and the hope of a greater approval. This "persecution" isn't something to ignore. It is real and effective in keeping us quiet and unengaged in sharing our faith with others. We desperately need liberation.

RECEIVING THE EMBRACE

When we are adopted into God the Father's family, we gain Christ's reputation — righteous, accepted, loved. God's holy opinion of us changes. Instead of "unacceptable," we become accepted. Instead of "unapproved," we become fully approved in Christ. The gospel of adoption reminds us that we have enduring approval before God the Father that cannot be matched by this world. God has infinitely more resources to love, accept, and show us that he approves of us. But to enjoy that reputation and gain the character to go with it, we have to give up our attempts at finding our approval in others. We have to give up putting our faith in what others think of us and humbly welcome what God the Father thinks of us. Like an adolescent child, squeamishly receiving his father's hug in public, we need to wiggle free from embarrassment. But there is no earning involved here. The Father's love is free and full. His approval is deep and enduring. His embrace is secure. When we are tempted to censor the gospel, we need to remind ourselves there is better acceptance found in Christ than in our circle of friends, neighbors, coworkers, and family members.

"The fear of man lays a snare, but whoever trusts in the Lord is safe" (Proverbs 29:25). If we live our lives in fear of what others might say or think about us, we will not truly live. We will live in a cage of fear, never sharing the gospel with others. But faith in Jesus liberates us from the cage so that we can find true safety in what the Lord thinks of us. The gospel releases us to run in the freedom of God's adopting love.

The gospel of adoption is the antidote to the idolatry of reputation. It frees us from what others think by releasing us into what God the Father thinks— *God*, the infinite, all-loving, truly glorious, humanity-restoring, grace-giving, personally attentive Savior and Lord. He looks at us and says, "You're accepted, loved; you're mine. Now go have fun, be yourself in Jesus, and when you have opportunity and prompting, tell others what I think of you in Christ."

Our own re-evangelization, as Christians, must precede our evangelistic efforts in the world. We need a fresh preaching of the gospel to idolatry-ridden hearts. Re-evangelization isn't merely a cultural need; it is a personal necessity. It isn't merely a period in church history, but a daily opportunity. We need to remind ourselves of the truth of

God's acceptance and approval in the gospel through regular meditation on Scripture, confession and repentance, community counsel, and worship. Obeying the mission of Christ and sharing your faith with others will lead to increased opportunities to confront your fear of man. The appropriate response is to run to the safety of Christ. Every fear, every embarrassment, every concern for our reputation can be matched by the approval and acceptance we find in the gospel. With the perceptions of others in check, we now turn to our perception of the gospel itself.

THREE-DIMENSIONAL GOSPEL

The gospel, when truly grasped in all of its richness and glory, will cause us to stop in our tracks, fall on our feet, and cry out to God in joyful worship or humble terror. When we pour over the "unsearchable riches of Christ," we discover that what God has done in Christ through the Spirit, and what he will do, has limitless applications to life. We possess the most attractive (and repelling) message on earth, which has been and should be communicated in endless dazzling (and mundane) ways in order to thrill the human heart, capture the imagination, and

> The gospel, when truly grasped in all of its richness and glory, will cause us to stop in our tracks, fall on our feet, and cry out to God in joyful worship or humble terror.

The gospel is the good and true story that Jesus has defeated sin, death, and evil through his own death and resurrection and is making all things new, even us.

rivet the intellect. Yet all too often, all we can eke out is a single phrase: "Jesus died on the cross."

What is the gospel? *The gospel is the good and true story that Jesus has defeated sin, death, and evil through his own death and resurrection and is making all things new, even us.* Staggering, isn't it? The gospel is both wonderfully simple and complex. It is simple enough for a child to grasp and profound enough that we will spend eternity pondering its beauty and its implications. Oliver Wendell Holmes once said: "I would not give a fig for the simplicity this side of complexity, but I would give my life for the simplicity the other side of complexity." In order to communicate the simplicity of the gospel, we need to grasp its biblical complexity. What does that mean?

Have you ever had the experience of seeing something familiar from a fresh perspective? Perhaps it's a work of art, or a new way of looking at an old picture, or even seeing someone you've known for years through the eyes of another person. The depth of our vision increases when we see something in multiple dimensions, from various perspectives.[3] Looking at the gospel from different perspectives, three dimensions emerge—historical, personal, and cosmic—revealing the height, width, and depth of the gospel. Taken together, these dimensions enable us to see a flat, simplistic story of a man dying on a cross in its full, three-dimensional beauty.

The historic, personal, and cosmic dimensions of the gospel are all embedded within the definition of the gospel given above:

- Historical — Jesus' true story of "death and resurrection"
- Personal — Jesus' defeating of sin and death for "even us"
- Cosmic — Jesus' overthrow of evil

Each dimension brings out an aspect of the good news that the other dimensions do not. They are mutually enriching and interpretive. The three dimensions are not three parts that can be separated from each other; they are three ways of looking at the gospel whole.

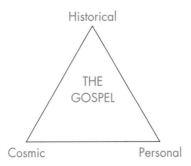

Jesus came preaching repentance and faith: "The time is fulfilled, and the kingdom of God is at hand; *repent* and *believe* in the gospel" (Mark 1:15, italics added).[4] The gospel is something that must be believed. When the Bible speaks of belief, it draws from Hebrew culture, where belief was a whole person phenomenon (heart, soul, and mind). In Western culture, belief is often relegated to the mind, a matter of intellectual assent. But when Jesus called people to believe the gospel, he called for a radical reorientation of not just their intellectual beliefs, but their personal devotion and life response.

In this sense, you could say that the preaching of the gospel calls a person to make *doctrinal, personal,* and *missional* changes. This threefold response mirrors the three dimensions of the gospel. Our doctrines change based on beliefs about history, our lives change based on beliefs about the person of Christ and what he has done for us, and our mission changes as we seek to renew our surroundings.

Historical gospel　⇨　changes doctrines

Personal gospel　⇨　changes people

Cosmic gospel　⇨　changes mission

Historical Gospel

The gospel is historical, Christ-centered, and newsworthy. The historical dimension emphasizes its doctrinal and theological content. It makes specific claims, which are grounded in historical events. In reminding the Corinthians of what is most important Paul writes: "Now I would remind you, brothers, of the gospel I preached to you.... For I delivered to you as of first importance what I also received, that Christ died for our sins in accordance with the Scriptures, that he was buried, that he was raised on the third day according to the Scriptures" (1 Cor 15:1–4). The vocabulary and structure of these verses indicate they were part of an early church tradition. Its rhythmic structure and essential gospel content made it both memorable and important to pass along. The tradition was likely formulated within one to two years after the resurrection of Jesus.

The gospel of "first importance" is a historical claim that Jesus Christ lived, died, was buried, and rose from the dead for our sins in the first century AD. Unlike other religions and philosophies, Christianity is rooted in particular events that occurred in history, namely, the life, death, and resurrection of Jesus. These claims must be believed in order to receive salvation. Because the gospel is historical—rooted in time and space—it is not just another spiritual idea or principle among many others. It is exclusive and unique in its claims (Acts 4:12; 1 Timothy 2:5–9), which demand to be accepted or rejected. Because God entered history, we have a strong reason for believing the gospel. *The historical nature of the gospel message changes what we believe.*

The gospel is centered on the person of Christ. It is not merely a historical event to be studied but a person to be worshiped. Through his incarnation, death, and resurrection Jesus permanently altered history, sending it in a redemptive direction. He opened up a way for humanity and creation to be reconciled to God. As a result, our faith should not be in doctrine but in Christ Jesus (2 Corinthians 1:20). Jesus, not doctrine, is the focus of the Scriptures. Charles Scobie helpfully focuses our attention on Jesus: "In the earliest days of the church Christians found their canon or norm not in writing, but in Christ himself, then in the gospel message that proclaimed the significance of the Christ event."[5]

The gospel is history-making news. We are told that Paul both received and preached "the gospel." The word gospel means "good news." It is the *announcement* of an event, not a mere statement of fact. And the gospel is news worth spreading. We recently had a slew of children born in our church. We recognized the significance of these new lives in our midst by announcing their births, celebrating the gift of new life. Births are so important they are worth public recognition and celebration! How much more is the news that Jesus has defeated sin, death, and evil through his own death and resurrection and is making all things new, including us.

The gospel is news worth announcing to the world, because it is news about Christ, who he is (his person) and what he has done (his work). The gospel addresses the problem of our sin and rebellion. How? Through the death and resurrection of Christ. In the gospel, we receive a promise from God that Jesus has redeemed us from our sin (Ephesians 1:7) and from the death penalty (Romans 6:23) for our crime of living a God-belittling life. Our faith is centered on Christ the person and what he has actually done, not on having the right doctrines or

The doctrinal gospel changes what we believe.

behaviors. The gospel reveals God to us uniquely, savingly, and gloriously in the person of Jesus Christ through the work of the Holy Spirit. Trusting this Person is what leads to salvation — not just believing a set of historic facts.

So we need to remember that doctrine is important, but it is just one dimension of the gospel. When we reduce the gospel to doctrines, facts, arguments, and Bible verses, we refuse to embody the humbling, personally transforming power of the gospel. Blinded by our longings to be right, we can easily become imbalanced. As a result, we may know the truth about Jesus but lack the power to personally change and lack an outward focus on loving others.

The doctrinal gospel is historical, Christ-centered, and newsworthy, but unless the other two dimensions complement it, we end up with a one-dimensional, "doctrinaire" gospel. This dimension of the gospel is foundational and primary, so I've placed it at the top of the triangle, forming the basis for the other two dimensions. If Jesus didn't truly live, die, and rise from the dead, then all of our attempts at personal change and social, cultural, and cosmic renewal are driven by human will, and they terminate on human glory. We then have no basis for true personal and social change (1 Corinthians 15:14–17), and we lose the very foundation of redemption.

Personal Gospel

A second dimension of the gospel, connected with the first, is the personal dimension. It tells us that the gospel *changes who we are.* The gospel is a *humbling, transforming message of grace.* It affirms human dignity by beginning our story, not with the fall or sin, but with creation and goodness. God made man and woman in his image and called us "very good" (Genesis 1:26, 31). As the story unfolds, this divinely bestowed dignity is traded out for man-made wisdom and glory. Satan sets the trap, but Adam and Eve willingly swipe at the bait. Desiring to take matters into their own hands, to secure godlike authority and wisdom, our first parents broke God's single command in the garden of his grace. As a result, man, creation, and the serpent are cursed.

The personal gospel changes who we are.

This historic act had sweeping consequences. The image of God was warped and the creation subjected to futility. The effects were (and are) devastating. Everyone is born into this fallen state, alienated from God. So while the gospel affirms our human dignity and worth, it is also painfully honest about our current status and desperate need. The gospel is offensive in this way because it tells us, in no uncertain terms, that we are dead people who need life, that we need to be changed, that we are rebellious creatures in need of either judgment or rescue.

Most reasonable people will agree that they need to change a few things. Consider your own life, the decisions you have made, and you'll probably be able to admit that some of your desires are bent and some of your thoughts are dark and selfish, even evil. We all need transformation. Yet something in our hearts doesn't want to admit this. We don't want to admit the full extent of our predicament before God, and because of this we are unable to receive God's gracious help. We need redemption, someone to set us free from our slavery to sin. The gospel is bold enough to tell us this, and that makes it a humbling message. Until we come to grips with our sinfulness and fully embrace the bad news of our condition before God, the gospel will remain a distant doctrine—not affecting us personally.

We all need change, but we just can't seem to change ourselves, which is precisely why we need God to change us. This is humbling, yes, but it is also freeing. It's freeing because the gospel is not about *us* changing us, but about *God* changing us. The gospel is the announcement that God will do what we cannot do for ourselves. He freely gives the Spirit of Christ to change us and make us new. He regenerates us:

> But when the goodness and loving kindness of God our Savior appeared, he saved us, not because of works done by us in

righteousness, but according to his own mercy, by the washing of regeneration and renewal of the Holy Spirit, whom he poured out on us richly through Jesus Christ our Savior, so that being justified by his grace we might become heirs according to the hope of eternal life. (Titus 3:4–6)

The word *regeneration* is a theological word that simply means to be reborn, to experience the generation of new life. And the only way we can permanently change is when the Spirit of God makes us new. Nothing else will last.

Near the conclusion of the movie *The Matrix* (1999), the main character, Thomas Anderson, is reborn. His guide and friend, Morpheus, shares with him the difficult news that he was born into bondage, trapped in a prison that he can't smell, taste, or touch. He is a slave, but he doesn't know it. He is deceived by his own senses, and the truth about his condition must be revealed to him. The only way out of this prison, the Matrix, is to be reborn, to undergo a transformation and become someone new (Neo).

At one point in the film, Anderson experiences a watery regeneration that results in his rescue. We, too, are imprisoned by something we can't smell, taste, or touch, the prison of our sinful nature, until we are rescued by Jesus and changed by "the washing of regeneration and renewal of the Holy Spirit." We need to acknowledge our sin, our need for rescue and regeneration, and place our hope and trust in Jesus to redeem and renew us. Jesus alone has the power to change us permanently. When Jesus makes us new, God no longer looks at us with holy disdain; instead, he sees us as new people, a part of his family, adopted through his Spirit and related to his Son. We enter communion with the Holy Trinity and join the family. Though once banned from soul-satisfying fellowship with the Father, the Son, and the Spirit, we are now free to walk with God in the garden of his grace.

The gospel changes what we believe, and it transforms who we are. The doctrine of the gospel, if we believe and cherish it, should lead to permanent and *continual* change. Once born by the Spirit, we begin to bear the fruit of the Spirit, things like love, joy, peace, faithfulness, and self-control (Galatians 5:23).[6] We suffer, work, celebrate, eat, and live differently. Why? Because the gospel does not give us mere doctrines to be believed, but introduces us to three Persons to be cherished. And the more we cherish them, the more they rub off on us.

As great and wonderful as it is to embrace and experience the personal dimension of the gospel, if we linger in our experience of personal change, we may end up neglecting the final aspect of the gospel — the missional dimension. If we aren't careful, we become well meaning, pietistic Christians who read their Bibles and pray, live moral lives, but do little for those around us. This imbalance produces inwardly focused Christians who are indifferent to the needs of those around them. Trapped in a great castle of like-minded people, we can't imagine the immense need outside our walls. Sometimes, we begin to see those on the outside as the enemy. Believing a two-dimensional gospel leads to selfishness and ends up drawing us away from Christ.

Cosmic Gospel

The three-dimensional gospel not only changes what we believe (doctrinal) and how we live (personal), but also *where* we live (missional). I realize that might sound a bit strange at first. In what sense can we say that the gospel changes *where* we live? If we believe the gospel, it must necessarily change how we interact and relate to the world. The gospel leads to changes in our surroundings because it calls us to join God's mission. We are called to love our neighbors, and this leads to the creation of great culture, the redeeming of social ills, and the sharing of the good news with others, inviting and teaching them to follow and obey Jesus. There are three aspects of the cosmic dimension of the gospel:

- Spiritual – sharing a whole gospel
- Social – redeeming social ills
- Cultural – making great culture

In his first public sermon, Jesus walked into a synagogue and read these words aloud from the scroll of the prophet Isaiah: "The Spirit of

The missional gospel changes where we live.

the Lord is upon me, because he has anointed me to proclaim good news to the poor" (Luke 4:18). In the Old Testament, prophets and kings were anointed with oil in recognition of their divine appointment. In Luke 3, we read the story of Jesus' baptism. At his baptism, Jesus isn't anointed with oil; instead, he is anointed with the one the oil represents—the Holy Spirit—who rests on him like a dove. His anointing is accompanied by a divine approbation from heaven: "You are my beloved Son; with you I am well pleased" (Luke 3:22). Yahweh declares that Jesus is not just a prophet and a king; he is his Son. No prophet or king had ever experienced this kind of anointing. What can we conclude from this? That this man is the much-awaited Messiah-King, the Son of God!

What is his mission? That question takes us back to Jesus' reading in the synagogue, to Isaiah 61. This was a well-known chapter among Jews because it promised the favorable day of the Lord, a coming age of spiritual, social, and cultural renewal. "The Spirit of the Lord is upon me, because the Lord has anointed me to proclaim good news to the poor ...

> [*Spiritual renewal*]
> to grant to those who mourn in Zion—
>   to give them a beautiful headdress instead of ashes,
> the oil of gladness instead of mourning,
>   the garment of praise instead of a faint spirit;
> that they may be called oaks of righteousness,
>   the planting of the Lord, that he may be glorified.
> [*Cultural renewal*]
> They shall build up the ancient ruins;
>   they shall raise up the former devastations;
> they shall repair the ruined cities,
>   the devastations of many generations.

Strangers shall stand and tend your flocks;
　foreigners shall be your plowmen and vinedressers;
but you shall be called the priests of the LORD;
　they shall speak of you as the ministers of our God;
you shall eat the wealth of the nations,
　and in their glory you shall boast.
Instead of your shame there shall be a double portion;
　instead of dishonor they shall rejoice in their lot;
therefore in their land they shall possess a double portion;
　they shall have everlasting joy.
[*Social renewal*]
For I the LORD love justice;
　I hate robbery and wrong;
I will faithfully give them their recompense,
　and I will make an everlasting covenant with them. (Isa 61:1 – 8)

After reading from Isaiah 61, Jesus makes an astounding comment. "Today this Scripture has been fulfilled in your hearing" (Luke 4:21). What is he saying? That he is nothing less than the Messiah-King, the Spirit-anointed one who has come to inaugurate the promised age of cosmic renewal!

This is the gospel that Jesus came to preach. A message of spiritual renewal: exchanging ashes of mourning for a headdress of rejoicing. A message of cultural renewal: for the repair of city walls, flourishing vineyards, and the possession of cultural treasures (wealth of the nations). And a message of social renewal: the undoing of injustice and sight for the blind (socially marginalized).

Jesus says he was anointed, not just to rule but to proclaim. The proclamation is of "good news," the Greek word *euangelion* that we translate *gospel*. Jesus was anointed to preach the gospel, to share the announcement that his reign will bring transformation for the poor, for the city, and for the spiritually captive. As the life and ministry of Jesus unfold, we see this happen. His gospel *was* good news for the physically and spiritually blind and poor.

All around us are people who live in spiritual darkness and physical

Jesus came preaching
a gospel of renewal.
A message of spiritual
renewal: exchanging
ashes of mourning for a
headdress of rejoicing.
A message of cultural
renewal: the repair of city
walls and possession of
cultural treasures. And a
message of social renewal:
the undoing of injustice
and sight for the blind.

poverty. We have the light, the means to *permanently* address the poverty and blindness of our cities. It is, to borrow a line from Tolkien, "a light to you in dark places, when all other lights go out."[7] The eternal light of the gospel is what chases the darkness away. Who are we to hide the light, to promote darkness, to keep people in poverty? This should compel us to listen to the broken-hearted, serve the needy, encourage the weak, and build up the city through making great culture and doing ethical work.

The gospel renews all things, socially, spiritually, and culturally, and will one day be completed for the people of God in the return of Christ.

The mission of God is made known to us in the person of Christ and is now assumed by the church through the Spirit *as we testify of the good news to the world.* We must take care that we do not restrict the implications of the gospel to just the historic and personal dimensions. Many evangelicals preach what Scot McKnight has called a "soterian gospel," one that exclusively focuses on personal salvation.[8] This kind of evangelism tends to restrict the implications of what God has done in Christ to the first and second dimensions of the gospel.

As McKnight rightly points out, personal salvation is just a subset of God's redemptive activity. God is also at work saving creation. God is a Creator who values the whole world, and he seeks to redeem it out from under the curse, which his Son Jesus Christ embraces by hanging on a tree (Genesis 3:14–19; Romans 8:18–25; Galatians 3:13; Colossians 1:20). Christ overthrows the curse by rising from the dead to liberate the world from its bondage and to restore repentant sinners to their glorious purpose as God's new humanity, the church, to participate in his grand agenda to make all things new (1 Corinthians 15; Revelation 21:5).

This is the gospel of the kingdom, and it has cosmic implications. God's kingdom is a realm of cosmic proportions stretching from city to city, country to country, planet to planet, from BC to AD. The cosmic gospel includes the redemption of humanity (the personal dimension) within God's larger agenda to redeem the whole world. As emissaries of Christ sent out into the world to announce the history-making news of the birth, life, death, resurrection, and return of Jesus, we must remember that this is news worth sharing. The gospel changes what we believe, who we are, and ... where we live.

ALL THREE DIMENSIONS ARE NECESSARY

What happens if we don't embrace all three dimensions of the gospel — doctrinal, personal, and social? Well, we end up with a one- or two-dimensional gospel. If we approach the gospel as just a *doctrine*, we become doctrinaire Bible thumpers. If we approach it just as a plan for *personal* change, we become closeted pietists, who have no good reason for what we believe. And if we approach the gospel as simply a *social message*, we turn Jesus into an activist. Before social and cosmic change is possible, our hearts must be transformed. If we aren't rooted in Jesus personally, we will burn out or blow up on socially minded self-importance, lacking a relationship with God. Eventually, we will kill ourselves, working to eradicate a curse that has been borne by the one who hung on a tree for us.

I hope you can see how important it is to affirm all three dimensions of the gospel. It's not a take-it-or-leave-it kind of thing. The gospel *is* three-dimensional. In order to avoid having an imbalanced gospel, we must seek God for the grace to live in the fullness of the gospel, not just in thirds. These three dimensions help us see that the gospel is eternal and unchanging, taking on many different shapes that draw out stunning truths that are hidden away until we uncover them. I call these truths *gospel metaphors*, a reference to the way the Bible describes enduring gospel truths in a variety of ways. Gospel metaphors can easily be used to communicate a gospel worth believing.

KEY QUESTIONS

1. What did the author mean when he said we put reputation before character?
2. Where are you tempted to do this?
3. Which of the three dimensions of the gospel are weakest in your discipleship?
4. If we are called to redeem social ill, make great culture, and share a whole gospel, which expression do you need to work on?

chapter seven

DIVERSITY: HANDLING THE GOSPEL IN ITS DIFFERENT FORMS

In the last chapter I gave a summary statement of the gospel and broke it down into three dimensions. In this chapter, we will look at how the Bible communicates the gospel through diverse metaphors, showing us different ways to handle the gospel. This will prepare us for part 3, where we will focus on specific methods for engaging in believable evangelism. Before we get to that, though, let's take a look at the evangelism of Jesus and Paul and unpack the five key gospel metaphors found in the New Testament.

THE EVANGELISM OF JESUS AND PAUL

Evangelism can include a variety of diverse speech forms, one of which is conversation.[1] We often prefer talking over listening, or we may listen but not really engage, failing to move to deeper areas. However, as we saw in chapter 2, Jesus was a good conversationalist. He asked questions that got below the surface, down into the heart. As a result, Jesus ended up communicating gospel truths in all kinds of ways. He was intentional in conversation, both as an active listener and a thoughtful participant.

Good conversation includes listening intently and speaking wisely. Listening well can lead to great insight about a person. Unless you know who someone is, it can be difficult to offer wise counsel.

Both Jesus and Paul were good conversatinalists. Let's consider Paul first. Acts tells us that Paul "reasoned" with Jews and Greeks (Acts 17:2, 17; 18:4, 19). We get our English word *dialogue* from this Greek word (*dialogizomai*), and while we must be cautious in drawing correlations directly from Greek to English, it is worth noting that Paul did not merely "preach" or herald the gospel, he also entered into thoughtful dialogue with non-Christians.[2] In Athens, he went to the synagogue and the marketplace every day to converse with the people there. We are told that "some of the Epicurean and Stoic philosophers also conversed with him" (Acts 17:18), and that people in the city spent their time "telling or hearing" something new. Whether engaging with religious Jews, philosophical Greeks, or everyday people in the marketplace, Paul listened, observed, and spoke.

Similarly, in a letter to Colossian Christian believers he wrote: "Walk in wisdom toward outsiders, making the best use of the time. Let your speech always be gracious, seasoned with salt, so that you may know how you ought to answer each person" (Colossians 4:5–6). Here Paul exhorts the Colossians to practice *personalized* evangelism, "that you may know how you ought to answer *each person*." When Paul spoke with people who were dead to God's saving grace, he respected the God-given gift of their intellect and recognized the importance of careful, culturally discerning speech. For Paul, evangelism wasn't just hit and run—preach the gospel and move on. He engaged in personal, attentive conversation with others. He got below the surface by asking meaningful questions.

Consider also Paul's use of Greek poetry and philosophy at Mars Hill (Acts 17:28) or his thoughtful use of the Greek word for "head" in Colossians. In the latter passage, Paul debunks Zeus as head of the cosmos and inserts Jesus as head, not only over the church, but over all things (Colossians 1:15–20). These evangelistic decisions are the result of someone who takes the time to think deeply about how to engage a culture. His insights likely developed as he used the powers of observation to listen and learn. Ruminating on these things helped him to participate in personal, relevant conversation with people. Paul worked hard to speak the gospel in meaningful ways.

In the city of Athens Paul intentionally chose to focus, not on the cross or forgiveness of sins, but on Jesus' resurrection and the coming day of judgment. Paul avoided the pressure of getting "the whole gospel" out in one hearing. He knew this was impossible. Instead, he carefully communicated a specific gospel metaphor, one he knew would rouse the interest of philosophers — the resurrection. Along with this, he spoke about a more familiar notion of divine judgment (Acts 17:22 – 31). Paul exercised discernment when communicating with people from different cultures and worldviews.

Like Paul, Jesus also listened and reasoned with people. He selected gospel metaphors appropriate for his hearers, using various images to communicate the hope of redemption and the kingdom of God. He used agricultural imagery with villagers (Luke 13), legal imagery with lawyers (Luke 11:37 – 54), spiritual birth with law-keeping Pharisees (John 3:1 – 8), and even water to share the good news with those who were thirsty (John 4:1 – 34). His gospel communication changed to suit

Paul avoids the pressure of getting "the whole gospel" out in one hearing. Instead, he carefully communicated specific gospel metaphors he knew would rouse interest.

his listeners' situation.[3] Jesus didn't use a canned presentation, but discerned how to best put the gospel into cultural idioms. This led him to draw on both creational and vocational imagery. Why go to such lengths to communicate a culturally discerning gospel if ultimately the work of salvation is entirely up to God?

People have reasons for not believing the gospel of Jesus, ranging from intellectual doubt to a failure to see any personal need for what Christianity has to offer. This is where Jesus-like evangelists come in. Joining the Spirit, we can roll up our sleeves, ask questions, and listen to begin the work of communicating a believable gospel.

Paul and Jesus were well aware of the condition of their listeners' hearts. Paul describes our hearts as darkened (Romans 1:21), boxed up in a coffin (Ephesians 2:1), dead and lifeless. Without the shining light of the gospel of the glory of Christ (2 Corinthians 4:4), darkened hearts aren't illuminated and dead bodies don't truly live. But the gospel that gives life to dead hearts isn't communicated in a vacuum. It's not a magical word from heaven that comes from nowhere. God chooses to work through means, and that means you and me. When we engage in mindless, impatient, and unwise evangelism, we are just piling stones on top of graves.

As I've interacted with homeless people over the years, I have been surprised to learn that many of them actually know the gospel quite well. They have heard it preached many times, but rarely does the message get personalized and applied to their heart. Good evangelism removes the stones and shares the truth in such a way that the light of God's grace can travel down a shaft, into the grave of a darkened heart. When we fail to address the reasons people have for not believing the gospel, we share an unbelievable gospel. We leave the stones in place.

People have reasons for not believing the gospel of Jesus, ranging from intellectual doubt to a failure to see any personal need for what Christianity has to offer. This is where Jesus-like evangelists come in. Joining the Spirit, we can roll up our sleeves, ask questions, and listen to begin the work of communicating a believable gospel. While God alone is the one who opens the heart, he uses us to prepare people to receive the message, to communicate it in a way that makes sense. This is why we must recover a way of communicating the gospel that embodies the gospel — patiently, wisely, and lovingly — revealing the beauty and believability of Jesus.[4]

GOSPEL METAPHORS

The Scriptures contain a variety of different ways of communicating the gospel, what we have been calling *gospel metaphors*. We have mentioned some of these already. These diverse expressions of the gospel allow us to communicate the good news in personal and contextual ways. These metaphors stretch across the breadth of the Bible, from Old Testament to New, collecting in the epistles where they are summarized in five distinct categories: justification, redemption, adoption, new creation, and union with Christ.[5]

Taken together, these gospel metaphors bring the full range of God's transformative grace to us in Jesus. But at the head of the five metaphors is our union with Christ. That union is what makes the metaphors meaningful and active in our lives. Apart from union with Christ, we cannot enjoy the riches of redemption, adoption, justification, and new creation. Of course, these four metaphors are also essential to our getting into Christ. Because of our union with Jesus, we receive an infinite supply of gospel graces. This is why I have chosen to depict the gospel metaphors with infinite, three-dimensional diamonds. The four sides depict each metaphor while the whole accounts for our union with Christ (see pages 140-41).

Though interrelated, each gospel metaphor conveys a unique blessing from the Father (Ephesians 1:3).[6] For example, justification helps us to see how a holy God can relate to sinful men and women, yet still remain holy. Justification explains how a righteous God relates to unrighteous people by declaring them righteous. But it doesn't do much to explain how we become part of God's family (adoption), how we receive and experience God's declaration of forgiveness and escape his wrath (redemption), or how we gain a new identity (new creation/regeneration).[7] All these metaphors stem from the same historic event — the life, death, resurrection, and ascension of Jesus Christ. They all communicate good news concerning Jesus and reveal how the Father, Son, and Spirit collaborate for our restored, renewed humanity. Impressively, these metaphors are also cosmic in scope, applying to the renewal of all creation.[8]

What exactly does each gospel metaphor mean? In the final section, I will show how each gospel metaphor uniquely speaks to a specific aspect of our human brokenness and sin. But first, here is a concise description of each. Study these descriptions, paying attention to how they differ from one another. Trust me, this will prove helpful as you begin the process of re-evangelization — thinking out *how* the gospel is good news:

- **Justification (legal metaphor).** This gospel metaphor resolves the dilemma of how a righteous God can relate to unrighteous people and still remain righteous. The solution is found in the person and work of Jesus Christ: "Yet we know that a person is not justified by works of the law but through faith in Jesus Christ" (Galatians 2:16). The good news of justification is that while our works are sorely inadequate, Christ and his work are infinitely sufficient for right standing before God. When we relocate our faith in him, we are drawn into his righteousness. *In short, Jesus is how a righteous God can relate to unrighteous people—by making us righteous. It deals with acceptance.*

  In Jesus, a righteous God relates to unrighteous people — by making us righteous.

- **Redemption (slavery and sacrificial metaphors).** This category of gospel metaphor deals with our otherwise incurable state as sinful and broken people. To redeem is to "set loose" from slavery to sin. Everyone needs redemption, but no one can free themselves. The price is too high—death is the sentence for the crime of our God-belittling lives. The only cure is for a God-sized person to take our place, absorb our sentence, and set us free. This happens in Jesus: "In him we have redemption through his blood, the forgiveness of our trespasses, according to the riches of his grace" (Ephesians 1:7). *In Jesus our incurable sinful status is uniquely cured—by absorbing our sin and death sentence. It deals with guilt.*

  In Jesus, our incurable sinful status is uniquely cured — he absorbs our sin and dies our death.

- **Adoption (familial metaphor).** This gospel metaphor changes our familial status before God, rescuing us out of Satan's family as "children of wrath" (Ephesians 2:3) and relocating us in the Father's family as "children of God" (1 John 3:1). This, too, happens through Jesus: "In Christ Jesus you are all sons of God, through faith" (Galatians 3:26). *In Christ, we are adopted out of the satanic family into God's family. It deals with approval.*

In Jesus, we are adopted out of the satanic family and placed into God's family.

- **New Creation (life and death metaphors)**. If justification changes our legal standing and adoption changes our familial status, then the new creation changes our spiritual nature. The language of the new creation speaks to matters of life and death. Though we are "dead in our trespasses," God makes us "alive together with Christ" (Ephesians 2:5). This new life is the eternal life imparted by the Spirit through the resurrected Christ. It is sometimes referred to as "regeneration" (Titus 3:5), which entails exile of the old life and birth of a new life within God's larger, cosmic work of new creation. *In Christ, the old nature is gone and a new nature has come—through his resurrection life. It deals with new life.*

In Jesus, the old life is exiled and a new life introduced—through his resurrection life.

Union with Christ (body-marriage metaphors). This final category of gospel metaphors serves as the integrating image by which we grasp the significance of all others. Without union with Christ, we gain no other gospel benefits. In Christ, we gain the world (1 Corinthians 3:22). However, our bedrock problem is that we are divided from Christ, unable to enjoy his grace, truth, and beauty—which is precisely why all saving benefits come to us through, in, and by Christ. By faith, we are drawn into inseparable spiritual union with Christ (Colossians 3:3) and receive the blessings of heaven (Ephesians 1:3). *Faith "in Christ" is the spiritual key that unlocks the storehouse of gospel riches—most of which is intimate relationship with Christ himself. It deals with intimacy and love.*

In Jesus, a life divided from God is united with him to enjoy all his graces.

Gospel metaphors are not symbolic of a deeper reality, but represent different facets of the one and only gospel, revealing its depth, complexity, and power.

Through faith in Jesus, God transforms us by his grace in many different ways. These are not metaphors in that they are symbolic of a deeper reality; they are ways of representing the reality of the gospel. They account for the depth, complexity, and power of the gospel; they are not different gospels. Though some might categorize these in different ways, I find it most helpful to focus on these five as the primary categories for understanding the gospel: justification, redemption, adoption, new creation, and union with Christ.

Each gospel metaphor can be used to talk about Jesus in ways that are culturally appropriate and personally meaningful. If you take the time to invest in learning and understanding each of these gospel metaphors and then listen carefully to people's stories, you will find yourself better able to discern how to communicate the gospel in a *believable* way. Your vocabulary of grace will increase, and you will become more fluent in the gospel. In each chapter of part 3, we will identify a single gospel metaphor accompanied by stories that narrate how to apply it, in a natural way, in a real situation with a real person.

KEY QUESTIONS

1. What surprised you about Jesus and Paul's approach to evangelism in comparison to modern forms of evangelism?
2. Start asking people more questions. Begin on the surface of life and move downward to heart matters of beliefs, feelings, and concerns of life.
3. Which gospel metaphors do you need to study further to understand them more clearly?
4. Begin thinking about how to apply a metaphor to a challenge you are facing.

chapter eight

FLUENCY: SPEAKING THE GOSPEL IN CULTURAL KEY

Now that we have a fresh vision of the gospel and different ways to handle its message, we turn to our speech. If our goal is to speak fluently about Jesus, it is imperative we understand the culture we are speaking to. This is precisely what good missionaries do when they move to a different country. They often take immersion courses to learn the indigenous language so they can communicate the gospel intelligibly. Cultural shifts in the West are so great and biblical illiteracy so vast that we must return to this missionary posture.

THE GOSPEL IN CULTURAL KEY

Cultural engagement is one of the reasons the early church was so successful at evangelism. They had a habit of getting into the mind-set of pagans and Jews alike to transpose the gospel into the appropriate key.[1] What does getting into the mind-set of non-Christians look like for us today? For many, the first step is figuring out how to escape our Christian ghettos. Living in the Christian subculture can make it difficult to know, much less engage, the non-Christians around us.

How can we escape our Christian ghettos? For starters, consider swapping out Christian versions of cultural activities. Instead of joining

The early church had a habit of getting into the mind-set of pagans and Jews alike to transpose the gospel into the appropriate key.

a Christian book club, join one at your local bookstore. Instead of playing church league sports, join the city league. Instead of inviting just Christian friends over for dinner, invite your neighbors over. When we engage those around us, we can begin to appreciate how they see the world and consider the audacious claims of the gospel from their perspective. This is an opportunity for us to grow and for the others to meet thoughtful, loving Christians who value different viewpoints on faith. Getting out of the ghetto and into the street will give us opportunities to learn what others believe and why they believe it, and to enter into thoughtful, respectful dialogue about Christ.

Once you get to know people who don't believe what you believe, you will have plenty of opportunities to transpose the gospel into a cultural key. As we learn more about people's objections to the gospel, we gain insight in how to talk to them in ways that make sense. This will vary with different cultures and subcultures. The gospel conversations I have in urban, countercultural Austin are very different from the conversations I once had in rural East Texas.

But you don't have to leave your city to begin transposing the gospel into a new cultural key. Each month, some of our city groups serve with Hope Street, a nonprofit on the east side of Austin. Through Hope Street, we are trying to show the mercy of God to the poor and marginalized at Booker T. Washington, Austin's oldest government housing. We gather kids from all over the projects by offering friendship and a nutritious meal, but first, they circle up to hear the gospel in Bible studies. All the kids are either African American or Hispanic, and many of them don't have fathers. Most know more about prison than I do.

One evening, as we were discussing the gospel, an eleven-year-old boy kept talking about his dad, who was in prison doing time. He shared about the drugs that had landed him there. His casual yet intimate knowledge of crime and the prison system was disturbing. The group leader, a man who had moved into the neighborhood to make disciples, was trying to explain *why* Jesus is essential for life. Thinking about the boy who had just shared, I jumped in and said to this him: "You know, the reason Jesus is so essential is that somebody has to take the bullet for what we've done. We have to go down and pay for the crime, unless there's someone who will take the bullet for us. That's what Jesus did. He took our bullet so we could be set free from our debt and be forgiven by a loving, just, heavenly Father."

I don't know if that explanation landed in his heart or not. I just know that I felt led by the Spirit to share it. Either way, I know that I would *never* have come up with that explanation of the gospel if I hadn't been in a different cultural context where guns, crime, and prison are part of everyday conversation. I was thinking in cultural key. This is what it means to walk wisely and respond to each person in their own

When the gospel intersects culture in a fresh way, it provokes worship because we get to see Jesus in a new light.

cultural context. When the gospel intersects culture in a fresh way, it provokes worship. We get to see Jesus in a new light. Thinking about this fresh expression of Jesus' sacrifice stimulated in me even more gratitude for the gospel. Each new cultural context affords fresh opportunities for theological insight, personal change, and increased gospel fluency.

MISSION IN POST-CHRISTENDOM

Cultural shifts have resulted in the collapse of Christendom, an official or unofficial relationship people have with their country and its civil religion. In many European countries, Christianity was the official civil religion, providing divine and moral guidance for governance. While America has a law separating church and state, Christianity was historically treated as the de facto faith of Americans. The Christian faith informed foundational documents of our government and laws, providing spiritual and moral guidelines for governance. This cultural Christendom is now collapsing, and the spiritual, ethical, and political fallout has begun.

In addition to loosening the American moral fabric, the collapse of Christendom leaves behind a rubble of theological understanding. As the dust settles, we can no longer assume that people know what words like Christ, sin, faith, and God mean. For many people, these words may no longer carry their original biblical meaning. As a result, the gospel gets lost in translation. For example, in secular culture people may actually hear us saying teacher (Christ), bad deeds (sin), wishful thinking (faith), or moldable deity (God). Today, it is a mistake to *assume* theological literacy. This is yet another reminder that we need to listen and ask questions as a part of re-evangelization. Missiologist Timothy Tennent suggests that the failure of Christians to ask and listen to new questions actually contributed to the collapse of Christendom.[2] If we are to move forward, the church must develop its ability to listen to new questions people are asking and learn how to translate the language of the gospel into words and concepts that speak to the heart.

We can no longer assume that people know what words like Christ, sin, faith, and God mean. For many people, these words no longer carry their original biblical meaning. We must transpose the gospel into their cultural key.

Let's drill down into another example, using the word "repentance." A clear goal in gospel communication is that people would respond in repentance and faith in Jesus, but that isn't always as simple as telling people to repent and trust Jesus (Mark 1:14–15; Romans 9:9). When I ask people what they think "repentance" means, I often hear unbiblical ideas, such as feeling really bad about your sins, being more moral to please God, or becoming spiritual. With this misunderstanding of repentance in mind, consider this story. A church planter in Austin planted little wire signs in grassy medians around the city that read "RepentAustin.org." I'll admit it's a pretty gutsy and confrontational tactic, but Jesus did call people to "repent and believe." Yet, as I thought about this evangelistic approach, one major objection I had was that these signs did not take into account contemporary understandings associated with the word "repent."[3] It likely conjured up images of judgmental people, filled with hatred toward "sinners," who self-righteously speak words of condemnation. I cannot imagine many Austinites found the signs endearing. Instead of intriguing people, it probably elicited disinterest and, perhaps, unduly promoted a distorted view of the gospel.

What makes this way of presenting the gospel distorted? First, it does not call attention to Jesus—it focuses on a person's need to change *before they even get to hear about Jesus and what he has done.* Second, there are strong cultural memories associated with the word, especially in Texas, that are connected with a return to good, moral living— again, a response that has nothing to do with Jesus and what he has done. Many Texas youths, when they hear the word "repent," associate it with things like: stop listening to secular music, stop sleeping with your girlfriend, and start going to church. This kind of repentance does not involve turning away from trusting in yourself to trust the Savior. It is simply a switch in lifestyles, secular to Christian. Mere moral reform has little to do with true repentance and faith in Jesus. You can alter your behavior without altering your savior. People adopt the trappings of faith—the religious habits, attempts at moral living, even a new Christianized culture that entails wearing a purity ring and listening to Christian music. But this cultural repentance is not a true turning to Christ; it is a turning to Christianity, to a religious subculture.

Good evangelists have to slow down long enough to understand what people hear and how they speak in order to communicate the gospel in intelligible ways. This involves listening to what people think in order to communicate meaningfully what God thinks. It involves listening to the questions people ask in order to ask them good questions, the questions God asks each of us. *This doesn't require a PhD in Bible or theology. It requires love: sacrificing our time, tweaking our crammed schedules, putting away our canned responses, and actually conversing with people.*

We have looked at a couple of examples of translating the gospel into a cultural and personal key. Part 3 will be filled with more of these. I hope you've caught the gist and got the bug to speak a more believable gospel. It's important that we move beyond namedropping Jesus or awkwardly inserting a reference to the death of a first-century Jew on a cross, devoid of any reference to a person's life and cultural context. People don't just need to hear a thirty-second gospel presentation. They need to understand *why* the gospel is worth believing. To do this, we must learn their language and know their stories. We need to become "culturally fluent," able to articulate the gospel personally in words and idioms that make sense to the people we talk to.[4]

KEY QUESTIONS

1. How can you adjust your lifestyle to engage more non-Christians and develop genuine friendships with them?
2. What are some ways that your friends and neighbors misunderstand Christianity? If you don't know, ask them what comes to mind when they hear the words: sin, Christ, faith, and God.
3. Think about a way to communicate these concepts that is both biblically accurate and culturally clear. Try doing it next time you talk to a friend.

03 METAPHORS

This section is represented by a four-sided diamond to symbolize the four gospel metaphors that all intersect to form a whole in our union with Christ. Its depth reminds us that there are endless gospel metaphors and infinite saving power packed into the gospel message.

This is the most practical section of the book. It is filled with examples of how to share a believable gospel by employing the five gospel metaphors. I have filled these pages with stories in the hope that they will stimulate your missional imagination, sparking ideas of how to better relate the gospel to others in your own life. These stories are also honest. They are messy, incomplete, and ongoing — just like real life relationships. All too often evangelistic training leaves reality out of the curriculum. I have tried to keep some of the real challenges of relationships in these stories. I hope they ring with authenticity, provide you with some helpful examples, and encourage you. I also pray that you will improve upon this section in your own life as you cultivate evangelistic wisdom and practice sharing a believable gospel.

chapter nine

SEEKING ACCEPTANCE

We all need to hear the gospel, the good and true story that Jesus has defeated sin, death, and evil through his death and resurrection and is now making all things new, even us. The challenge of evangelism is to take this sweeping, cosmic gospel and communicate it to the "even us." People need to know *why* Jesus is worthy of their faith.

One of the greatest needs people have today is to be accepted, to know that they are welcome and won't be rejected. Though we may try to deny or hide it, we all carry with us a sense of shame, a fear that we will be found out, rejected, and judged when people learn who we really are. In order to be accepted, people fill this vacuum in various ways. Some try to earn their acceptance, while others try to downplay their need by hardening themselves. This often happens by trying to fill the need by running from relationship to relationship or from achievement to achievement, seeking acceptance from others, self, or even God.

JUSTIFYING THE RELIGIOUS SECULARIST

My wife, Robie, met Andrea in BookPeople, a local indie bookstore. The fabric of Andrea's dress caught Robie's eye—it was identical to the fabric she was working on at the time. As a seamstress, my wife notices these things, something most of us wouldn't. I love that God uses our personal interests to open doors for relationship and conversation with others. Robie struck up conversation with Andrea and quickly learned that she was going through a difficult time. Andrea mentioned, in passing, that she knew "the universe had an answer" despite the troubles in her life.

One thing led to another. They exchanged emails and talked about getting together with their kids. Soon, Andrea and her kids started coming around for birthday parties, weekend hangouts, and play dates. Eventually, Andrea thought it would be nice for her husband to meet us,

One of the greatest needs people have today is to be accepted, to know that they are welcome and won't be rejected. Though we may try to deny or hide it, we all carry with us a sense of shame, a fear that we will be found out, rejected, and judged when people learn who we really are.

and she suggested bringing him to church on Sunday.[1] Being a discerning and caring person, Robie let her know that this wasn't necessary and invited the family over for dinner instead. Why pass up an opportunity to get the family to a church service? Privately, my wife told me that she didn't want Steve to meet me as a "preacher" — she wanted him to know me first as a regular person.

We enjoyed a great night together. It was great to finally meet Steve, and soon afterward we began connecting for lunch on a regular basis. Eventually, he and his family did begin attending our Sunday church gatherings, and Steve heard the gospel regularly preached. He began connecting with others in the church.

With a theater background, Steve was passionate about acting and had tried running his parents' company, but he was now selling insurance, trying to make ends meet. He had some Jewish roots, but was now more agnostic in his beliefs. Yet over time, he began changing. He initiated family prayer at dinnertime, started reading books about the gospel, and even attended a few of our City Group meetings. Steve had plenty of exposure to the gospel — through sermons, church relationships, books, and the like — so, naturally, I was curious to know where he was with Jesus. I invited him out to lunch and brought along another guy I was discipling.

We ordered our food and engaged in some chitchat. Then I asked Steve where he was at in his faith: "So, Steve, how are things with Jesus?" He responded by describing some of the challenges he was facing, both financial and spiritual. He remarked: "I'll never be like my moral superior at work. I'm just trying to climb that spiritual ladder, man; but I'm just not doing that well. But I am *trying*." As I listened, I could empathize with his struggles. I suggested some alternative options for employment since his sales commissions just weren't coming in, and then I looked him directly in the eyes. I wanted him to know that despite his struggles, he had a friend who was there for him, someone who would listen. Then I asked him a question: "Steve, would it be alright if I picked up on a couple things you said about your spiritual struggle? I noticed that when I asked you about how things were going with Jesus, you described your moral superior at work and the difficulty of climbing the spiritual ladder … I really admire your effort, but I've got some bad news: you'll never be moral enough for a perfect, holy God."

I continued. "You aren't the only one. I could never be moral enough either, but the good news is that Jesus climbed down that spiritual ladder to die for our moral failures. He died to forgive you for not being moral enough. Then, being morally superior to all of us, he promises to put you on his back and carry you up that spiritual ladder to place you in front of a holy God, fully loved and fully accepted. That, Steve, is what Jesus has to do with your life."

I wasn't sure how Steve would respond. But there was a look of wonder on his face as we talked. He looked right at me and asked: "Is it really that easy?" I had to pause a minute to think about my answer. "Yes, it really is that easy. Give up on yourself and give in to Jesus. God is offering you perfect acceptance. It's called grace."

"Is it really that easy?" I had to pause a minute to think about my answer. "Yes, it really is that easy. Give up on yourself and give in to Jesus. God is offering you perfect acceptance. It's called grace."

As I listened to him, one need in Steve's life kept surfacing. It wasn't his financial needs; it was a spiritual need, a need for acceptance. Steve had heard me preach, he had read Christian books, and he had been involved in our community. But he still didn't see how the gospel uniquely addressed his heartfelt needs. He may not even have been aware of his need. But what he needed was acceptance, and he needed to hear the gospel through the lens of *justification*.

Recalling our explanation from chapter 8, justification answers the question: "How can a righteous God relate to unrighteous people and still remain righteous?" Paul's letter to the Romans is the classic text on justification. By chapter 3, he establishes that "none is righteous, no, not one" (Romans 3:10). Steve was aware of his unrighteousness, which is why he was working hard to make himself "right" enough for God. His nagging sense that he wasn't good enough for God was right, but his solution was wrong. I knew this because I was familiar with the gospel of justification, *and* I was listening carefully to what he was saying.

This gospel metaphor isn't the immediate answer to everyone's struggle. As we will see, others need to hear the gospel explained in a different way. But I knew Steve had a hard time fitting in socially, vocationally, and now spiritually. He was no longer working for his parents, and he was trying to prove himself, but his motivation was bottoming out. His desire to prove himself had shifted, and he was trying to please God, to earn his acceptance. Justification was the gospel chord that needed to be plucked.

I didn't want to diminish his sincere efforts or discourage him. After all, he had made some significant shifts over the past months. However, his effort would never be enough before God. Paul explains, "For by works of the law no human being will be justified in his [God's] sight" (Romans 3:20). Whenever we try to justify ourselves to someone in an argument, we try to prove that our position is right and should be accepted. When arguing with a perfect Judge, whose holy character demands perfection, it is downright impossible for anyone to justify their position.

We simply can't make the case that we are perfect, nor can we do enough good to warrant an acquittal. Therefore, we must pay for our offense. We must do the time. The punishment must fit the crime. Failure to live up to the infinitely righteous standards of an eternal God results in an infinite and eternal punishment—unless, someone who is eternal and infinite serves our sentence. This is precisely what Jesus did: "[we] are justified by his grace as a gift, through the redemption that is in Christ Jesus" (Romans 3:24). Jesus steps in to die our deserved death; that's grace. Jesus redeems our position by paying our price. His death is our freedom. His resurrection life results in our acceptance (4:25). As a result, anyone who banks on him (believes in him) is acquitted. Not only that, such a person is also made right with God. God remains a just judge, the sentence is carried out, and we are justified before him in Jesus (3:26). It's the deal of history!

It was obvious that Steve didn't understand this because when asked about Jesus, his first thought wasn't about what Jesus had done for him, but what he could do for Jesus—his attempts to climb the "spiritual ladder" and his need to "try harder." How does the gospel free him from this struggle to prove himself to God? The answer was obvious! Using Steve's language and responding to his struggle, I tried to show him the futility of his self-righteousness by communicating the hope of a *different* righteousness. He needed to be incorporated into what Jesus had done for him, not isolated in his own efforts to please God. Steve didn't have to prove himself to God because Christ has proven himself enough for him. He could be freely accepted by a righteous God because of Christ's righteous sacrifice and resurrection on his behalf (Rom. 4:25).

Steve struggled with the same thing that many people struggle with—engaging in religious performances to merit God's acceptance. It was clear to me that Christ's performance on his behalf was precisely what he needed. I could have shared the gospel in a variety of ways, picking up on the metaphor of redemption or new creation, but after listening I discerned that the notion of justification would likely mean the most to him. By applying the gospel of justification to his struggle of moral and spiritual performance, I was able to make an unbelievable gospel believable. The gospel was believable for Steve because he saw

The hope of justification is that we can be perfectly and completely accepted by the one who matters most — God the Father.

how the good news immediately answered his need. It was truly good news for his bad news.

There are millions of people like Steve, people who are working hard to earn their acceptance in society. This includes progressive, secular people like Steve, but it also includes many who attend church and live "religious" lives. Steve was immersed in our church community for a while, a community that preaches justification by faith in Christ, and yet he was still driven to perform. His drive wasn't changed by his surroundings, or even by the things he did. It came out of his heart. He had a primal need to make something of himself, to count, to make his life a success on his own — and receive the credit for his efforts. Not everyone is searching for acceptance in the same way, and justification may not jive with them in the way it did with Steve. Tim Chester helpfully breaks down several ways people attempt to justify themselves:[2]

- proving yourself to yourself
- proving yourself to others
- proving yourself to God

Each of these efforts to find acceptance has a different target: self, people, or God. As we have seen, our efforts are not enough. The acceptance we all seek cannot be found in anyone other than God. He alone offers enduring acceptance and perfect love. The hope of justification is that we can be perfectly and completely accepted by the one who matters most — God the Father. Because of Jesus, we need not lift a finger to prove ourselves to God and now have every reason to live our whole lives with and for him.

If you listen closely, you may hear desires for acceptance in the hearts of others, or you may not. This isn't the most pressing felt need for everyone. People who have different felt needs may need to hear a different gospel metaphor in order to be transformed by the truth. Nevertheless, it is important to understand the unique way in which justification makes unrighteous people right with a righteous God. It is good news we all need to hear, especially those seeking an enduring acceptance.

KEY QUESTIONS

1. Do you know anyone seeking acceptance? How can you offer them the hope of justification in Christ?
2. What are some other ways people seek acceptance? How is Jesus better than that object or person?
3. What is your next step with this person?
4. Begin praying that they will wake up to God's acceptance in Christ.

chapter ten

SEEKING HOPE

The metaphor of new creation can be especially compelling for people who are longing for a new start in life. People whose lives have been littered with failure, scarred by abuse, humbled through suffering, or ruined by addiction need the hope of becoming a new creation. The hope of the new creation appeals to anyone who senses that they have been living in sin before a holy God and who long to escape from their old life of sin to experience the freedom of new life in Christ. Paul describes our new creation hope in this way: "Therefore, if anyone is in Christ, he is a new creation. The old has passed away; behold, the new has come" (2 Corinthians 5:17).

Reading closely, this passage tells us how we experience this *new creation* life. It happens "in Christ," through being united with Christ. The new creation is the result of Christ "reconciling us to himself" (redemption), which through faith leads to our becoming the "righteousness of God" (justification). This is a great reminder that the gospel metaphors don't exist independent of one another. Instead, they work together like the different sections of an orchestra to create the symphony of salvation. Still, there is great value in learning which gospel chord to pluck. Different gospel metaphors resonate with people, depending on where they are in life. Sometimes, someone's need sits right on top of their story, like Ben.

NEW HOPE FOR BEN

I first met Ben at a house that had been converted into a state rehab center. As I approached the 1980s-style, one-story building, I quickly realized the gravity of the moment. Met by an armed officer, I was told to leave all my personal belongings behind. After registering and watching an advocate video, I was released to talk to Ben. We went outside to talk. The ground was parched, sparsely populated by bits of grass struggling to grow in the thick Texas heat. There were a few trees on the grounds, providing occasional relief from the sun. Ben made his way over to a round, cracked, stone table and sat down on the bench. The cemetery-like outdoor furniture was foreboding. Stale cigarette smoke hung in the air as I joined Ben, sitting on the bench across from him.

Bloated and nervous he looked at me. I opened our conversation by thanking Ben for agreeing to meet with me. After some small talk, I asked Ben to tell me his story. "Ben, I know this isn't the script you wrote for your life. It's not what you dreamed of as a kid. Tell me how you got here. I want to hear your story."

Reaching back to his childhood, Ben shared several experiences of rejection in close relationships. He had been adopted as a child and

People whose lives have been littered with failure, scarred by abuse, humbled through suffering, or ruined by addiction need the hope of a new creation.

often felt out of place; he felt as if he didn't belong. Ben talked about feeling different, not accepted by others, and he carried around a deep sense of loneliness. Drugs had offered him an escape from this feeling and introduced him to a new, more accepting community of users. Somewhere along the way, he discovered that their community was more about sharing their "highs" than sharing life together. There were limits to their acceptance. Aware that his drug community wasn't a place where he was safe, Ben tried to numb his pain with even more aggressive drugs.

Before he knew it, ten years of his life had flown by. Now he was sitting in front of me in rehab, on probation, sharing his life story with a pastor he had met only once before. Ben had been raised in the church, and he could tell me who Jesus was, but he had never found the gospel truly believable. Growing up, he had been told that Jesus died on the cross for him, but his experience in the church had been one of rejection, not acceptance. Because he had never experienced true acceptance with God's people, he had concluded the gospel wasn't something really worth believing. Rejecting Christ, he moved toward atheism.

As I listened to Ben, I kept asking myself and praying: *How can I talk about Jesus in a way that meets Ben where he is right now? What do I tell him, a broken, lonely, anxious, and recovering addict? Do I repeat what he has heard before: "Don't worry, Ben, just believe Jesus died on the cross and everything will be okay"?*

Ben clearly needed more than just a few memorized facts about Jesus. He needed someone to help him understand how the person and work of Jesus could actually make a difference in his life. As these questions tumbled in my mind, I became immediately aware of one thing: Ben had a deep need for hope. Yes, Ben's story was one of searching for acceptance, but the message he was sharing with me was a story that lacked hope. Ben had been through hell and back as an addict, and now he was worn out, at the end of his rope, and ready for a new start. Name-dropping Jesus wouldn't cut it. He'd heard that before. He needed to see and feel the radical promise of the gospel. Instead of *correcting* his life choices, I needed to *understand* his life choices. So sitting there with him, I asked him a number of questions:

"When the church rejected you, did you experience rejection from your parents also? How did that make you feel?" Ben made it clear that his parents were good people. He was equally clear that he didn't like the church. I asked him why, and he said that he felt as if the people there didn't really accept him. He felt like they were always talking about him.

"What was your drug community like?" Ben shared that he felt accepted by the other users until he would try to stop using. Then, they would give him a hard time. His acceptance with them was conditional, only offered when he was also using.

"What were you looking for in all of this?" Ben thought about it but admitted that he didn't know.

"If you could have anything right now, what would it be?" At this, Ben gave me a clue that he hadn't given up yet. He said that he wanted to get out of rehab and start putting his life back together.

I asked Ben these questions because I cared about him. I wasn't following an evangelistic formula or reading the questions off a checklist. This was a budding relationship with a fellow human who was clearly struggling to make sense of his life. I expressed empathy, concern, and compassion. I searched my mind for what to say that might be worth believing for Ben. I could have just as easily picked up on his longing for acceptance and shared the gospel of justification or talked about his need for belonging and intimacy through the lens of adoption, especially since he was an adoptee, but there isn't a magical formula that you need to apply each time.

Instead, I was praying throughout our conversation for the Spirit to lead me. Despite some of the other ways I could have talked about the gospel, I sensed a strong urge to follow up with Ben on the hope of the new creation. I knew that even though Ben longed for acceptance and approval, those longings were deeper, further back in his story. What I was hearing on the surface was his desperate need for hope. Ben wasn't looking, in that moment, for answers to his need for acceptance or intimacy; he wanted to know whether it was possible to escape the drug-distorted way of living and start a new life.

I asked Ben these questions because I cared about him. I wasn't following an evangelistic formula or reading the questions off a checklist. This was a budding relationship with a fellow human who was clearly struggling to make sense of his life.

I asked Ben, "What have you been searching for?" He talked about his loneliness and disappointment. I asked him how he thought God might figure into those longings, and he admitted that he wasn't sure. I sensed that he was tired of his old life, that he wanted to escape his broken, cemetery life and get a new start. He wanted to believe that a brighter future was possible, but that hope was buried and faint. Ben needed to hear the gospel of new creation.

I knew that the promise of new creation could make the gospel more believable for Ben. He was longing to know if there was grace that could remedy his past failures and remake him into a new man. A cloud of skepticism hung over his story, but at the risk of rejection, I tried sharing the new creation hope of the gospel: "Ben," I said, "I know you're tired and worn out. I know this isn't what you hoped for your life and I want you to know that God loves you. He wants to *make you new*. He wants to exile that old life and *give you a new life* in Jesus. Jesus died to give you this life, to forgive you and shower you with his grace. He wants you to come back home to enjoy his love, acceptance, and peace. Instead of trusting in the escape of drugs and the fleeting acceptance of a drug community, he wants you to trust in Christ to become a new creation, to *be remade from the inside out*. How does that sound?"

As we talked, Ben considered what I was saying. There were no fireworks, no spontaneous baptism, but that didn't bother me. I knew the Spirit was at work and that evangelism is a process. Ben admitted that he wasn't even sure if he still believed in God. So we talked about his struggle to believe, and I invited him to trust Christ with his doubts. I told him that God and I were okay with him doubting, but that he needed to test his doubts. I asked if he would be willing to read the Bible and talk to God about it. He said he would, so I gave him a Bible and we prayed.

Ben's addictions ran deep, and he needed a deep gospel. A shallow gospel presentation wouldn't cut it, not with what he'd been through. A simple invitation to try harder or blindly trust Jesus would fall on deaf ears. Having heard many times that Jesus had died on the cross for his sin, I knew repeating the same information wasn't what he needed. Ben would probably screen it out and dismiss it. Instead, he needed to hear how the gospel is good news to him, why Jesus' death makes a difference in his life. He needed to know that the Bible spoke to his longings, his hopes for a new life. I shared with him that his old man could be exiled

New creation promises to rectify us with God and the world, alleviating despair and injecting hope into the human heart.

and a new man could emerge (1 Corinthians 5:17–18; cf. Galatians 6:15; Ephesians 4:20–24; Colossians 3:9–10). Ben needed a believable gospel.

Two years later, Ben stood up in one of our Sunday church gatherings. He was no longer bloated. His teeth had been repaired. Physically, he looked like a new man, but that wasn't the reason for the hope shooting out of him. Calm and composed, Ben stood before our church family and kicked the doors off his private struggles, sharing the story of his addiction and recovery. You could hear a pin drop in the room that morning. Ben shared his struggle to find meaning and acceptance. We asked him to share what had changed in his life, and Ben spoke of his faith in Jesus: "Now, I believe," he said. "I have received God's grace, I know that I'm forgiven for all I've done, and I know that God wants to know me." Ben has replaced his addiction to drugs with a growing addiction to grace.

We also asked Ben to share how, specifically, he has experienced the grace of God. He responded by speaking of the gospel of new creation: "being able to start new." For Ben, God's grace has meant a new life, a complete change from his old life. He spoke about his old way of living: "It seems like such a long time ago … I feel like that person is way in the past … it amazes me that I could have grown so much in a year and a half." By grace, Ben sent his old man into exile and became a new man in Christ! Belief in the gospel of new creation made Ben new. The hope of new creation resonated with his longings, pulling him to trust Jesus. As he turned toward Christ, Ben experienced sorrow for his sins and joy for his forgiveness. He has now moved away from rejection and has found deep acceptance and love in Christ. Ben now spends his time baking for others, keeping the prayer list for his community group, and caring for his grandparents. I've learned so much about what it means to be a new creation from watching Ben change.

ONE GOSPEL METAPHOR IS NOT ENOUGH

Ben's story isn't over. Each day he continues to work out his new life in Christ, and like all of us, he is often tempted to return to his life of exile. God does not demand perfection overnight; that's what Christ is for. Instead, he calls us to a persevering faith over a lifetime. Getting *to* Christ and then persevering *in* Christ requires more than one gospel metaphor. As Ben's struggles with sin continue, as his relationships change, and as his life in Christ grows and matures, he will need different expressions of the gospel, different gospel metaphors applied to his life. We need *all* of the benefits of Jesus' life, death, resurrection, and reign, and different elements of the gospel will be more compelling and necessary to us at different points in our discipleship. In this short account of Ben's life, we saw elements of redemption, justification, adoption, and new creation.

There are struggles and hopes, fears and dreams that sit on the surface of our stories. When we talk with people, we need to do the loving, patient, and discerning work of listening well to their stories. Most importantly, we must prayerfully listen with dependence on the Holy Spirit. As we do this when we talk with people, different gospel metaphors may begin to surface, helping us to discern how the good news is good in their bad news, enabling us to communicate a believable gospel.

KEY QUESTIONS

1. Do you know anyone like Ben? Can you think of other kinds of people that might be seeking hope?
2. Can you think of other metaphors related to new creation?
3. What are some other ways to communicate hope to the hopeless?
4. Do you know anyone who needs to hear about the hope of new creation?

chapter eleven

SEEKING INTIMACY

In the film *Her,* Joaquin Phoenix plays Theodore, a lonely writer who develops a relationship with his operating system, Os1. The film is set sometime in the near future, and Os1 is sentient, emotive, and personal. Her name is Samantha, and she's got the sultry voice to go with it (narrated by Scarlett Johansson). Theodore is not a hermit. He has real relationships and interactions. He can hold conversations with people and by all appearances, he functions perfectly fine in everyday life. But as the movie reveals, what he longs for most, intimacy and love, he is only able to find in an alternate reality, in *Her.* As absurd as the story sounds, it is far more common than you might think. People everywhere are seeking intimacy.

Most of the time we seek intimacy in actual relationships with other people. Occasionally, we discover a relationship that is deeply fulfilling, but no matter whom we connect with there is eventually disappointment. All too often, after experiencing disappointment we respond by packing up and moving on. One by one, we cross people off our intimacy list: parents, friends, significant others, and spouses. It's no wonder the divorce rate is so high. But the search for deep intimacy isn't restricted to marriage. Thirty-seven million singles between the ages of twenty and forty are delaying marriage. Many of these "never-marrieds" practice serial monogamy in their steady search for intimacy.[1]

Occasionally, we discover a relationship that is deeply fulfilling, but no matter whom we connect with there is eventually disappointment.

Our search for intimacy is revealed in other relationships as well. In our friendships we long for a sense that we belong, for a place where we can be ourselves and know that we are accepted. We want relationships that are secure, where we feel safe to share our innermost thoughts and darkest struggles.

Christians are no exception to this. Unfortunately, in their search for intimacy many Christians practice serial monogamy with churches, going from church to church until they finally give up and leave. They are on a search for that perfectly accepting community, the one that will never disappoint them. John was on a search like this when I met him.

I first met John at the Highball, a swanky retro bar with classy bowling, karaoke rooms, a large wooden dance floor, and a wide selection of infused liquor. The booths and chairs are upholstered in sparkly gold plastic, kind of like those gold motorcycle helmets or a glittered bowling ball. The Highball is the kind of place where Frank Sinatra would hang out. As a church, we gathered there on Sundays to worship God and engage our city. On this particular Sunday, John walked through the door, cynical and searching. A sign hung over his heart that read: "Do not enter." As I talked with him, I learned that he had some childhood experience with church, but he had never been thrilled by the gospel. He was there that morning to give "church" another try.

Over the next few months, John became more involved in our church community. He liked the idea of church as more than just a service on the weekend. He appreciated that we were about relationships, connecting throughout the week and being involved in one another's lives on a regular basis. His culinary skills wooed many of us to join him for some great gatherings. It was clear that John loved connecting with other people. He even invited us to join him in reaching out to the community through an annual Olympics event for the handicapped and elderly. A number of us volunteered with him for that event, and it seemed like John was really growing.

There was one problem with his growth, however. John was growing attached to the church, but he wasn't growing attached to Christ. Without Christ, there is no power to change, no way to truly grow into a new person. He developed an unhealthy attachment in these relationships, looking for them to provide a level of intimacy and attention that only God can provide. If some people didn't turn out for one of his parties, John would complain about them. He would accuse people of being hypocrites and talk about how everyone else was letting him down. His needs shifted over to one of our pastors who was discipling him. He became so attached to the pastor that he'd call constantly for help, and he expected our pastor to leave his family and drop everything to counsel him. If the pastor didn't respond in the way John liked, the pastor got thrown under the bus too.

Despite deep, Christ-centered counseling, extended phone calls, and lots of prayer and community, John refused to replace his god of intimacy with Jesus. His constant need for intimacy began to drain his wife as well, who had grown cool to his "Do not enter" attitude. John's need for intimacy, for security in his relationships, had become a god to him. He was placing deity-sized expectations on ordinary humans, and none of us would be able to live up to them — not the church, not his pastor, not even his own wife. Sadly, his wife ended up divorcing him. His idol devoured him, and he drifted away from our church.

We have all been created by God with a capacity for intimacy and love, but that capacity was never intended to be completely satisfied by

Our therapeutic culture reinforces the idea that we deserve to have all our longings fulfilled by others. These good, deep longings — to know others and be known without fear of rejection — can only be met by someone big enough to fulfill them.

individual human beings. Unfortunately, our therapeutic culture reinforces the idea that we deserve to have all our longings fulfilled by others. These good, deep longings we all have—to know others and be known without fear of rejection—can only be met by someone big enough to fulfill them. When those needs are not met and we demand them from others, we end up accusing and angry, or withdrawn and depressed. The idol of intimacy surfaces in these two ways. John tried walking both the demanding and the depressed paths, and as a result, his life became a relentless game of push and pull. He refused to repent of his idolatry and surrender his longings to Christ. Instead, his healthy longings for relational intimacy became life-destroying demands. The good news tells us that there is only one relationship that can bear the weight of our inordinate desires for intimacy and love—union with Christ.

Union with Christ is, as it sounds—a deeply personal, affectionate relationship with Christ. It involves a change in our relationship with Christ that is covenantal and spiritual, and it affects the way we relate to God, the way we relate to others in the "body" of Christ, and how we see ourselves (our identity). It is a relationship that is entirely dependent on what Christ has done for us—his life, suffering, dying, rising, and ascending in order to draw us to be with him and to enjoy perfect love, acceptance, and divine intimacy. In Christ, we are hidden in God's divine love, no longer judged or treated on the basis of our own faults, failure, and sins (Colossians 3:1–4). Because we are treated as one with Christ, mystically incorporated into the person of Christ, we gain an entirely new identity.

The many "in Christ" statements littered throughout Scripture unpack what this union means for us, both individually and collectively as the people of God. Ephesians 1 shows us that all of the heavenly blessings come to us "in Christ Jesus" (1:3). In other words, we never stand before God alone, apart from Jesus. These blessings includes our election (God's choosing of us), our receiving grace (God's unmerited favor), our redemption (God's saving us from the consequences of our

The good news tells us that there is only one relationship that can bear the weight of our inordinate desires for intimacy and love — union with Christ.

sin), our reconciliation (God's restoring us to right relationship with him), our forgiveness (God's not counting our sins against us), and our sealing by the Spirit (God's power to change us and make us his forever). The gospel metaphor of union with Christ is foundational, the means by which all of God's blessings are given to us. It is the essential doctrine through which all other saving doctrines flow.

Knowing that we belong to Christ leads to profound shifts in the way we think about ourselves and our relationships with others. Instead of an opportunity to demand our rights or to hide from others, we begin to see relationships as a way of growing in our love for God. We experience God's grace and encounter Christ as we serve others and are served by them. This is what we tried to explain to John. We saw his longing for intimacy and tried to connect it with the truth that in Christ we no longer need to seek to have all our needs met; instead, we are free to serve others. This wasn't just a single conversation. We spent a lot of time with John, enjoying his parties, suffering through his stinging remarks, serving alongside him in outreach, and praying and listening to him. In a sense, we also modeled the truth of union with Christ to him.

Sharing a believable gospel isn't as simple as seeing what someone needs and telling them about it. Ultimately, the gospel needs to connect with the heart through the supernatural work of God's Spirit. We shared our insights, walking with John down the long road of relationship. God asks us to love imperfect people, imperfectly, over time. As we did with John, we discerned this pattern—the push/pull of his longing for intimacy—and we surfaced it for him through good questions. We asked him questions like:

Do you see the pattern of broken relationships in your life?
Why do you think those are there?
Is it possible that your expectations for intimacy have become demands?

In talking about this, John would often grow angry. He would complain that reading his Bible didn't lead to a *feeling* of closeness. This is an objection many raise. There are times when our emotions don't always match our intimacy. I am very close to my wife; we are committed to one another and our relationship is secure, but I don't always *feel* close to her. The Bible and prayer are means of grace to draw near to God and to orient our trust in him. They aren't magic lamps we rub to get an emotional connection. Fortunately, the Lord does give us times of intense emotion, but even these are rarely perfect experiences, and they certainly don't last. Our relationships are still affected by the reality of sin, and we are prone to elevate them above God. That's what we were trying to help John see. In the end, his actions and demands were affecting his relationships with others, but ultimately, his sin was against God. By consistently choosing to look to others to meet his needs instead of trusting God to meet them, he was rejecting God.

After several months of conversation, John reluctantly agreed with us. He knew, at least rationally, that Christ was his only hope, but he was so devoted to his idol of intimacy that he just couldn't let it go. He wasn't ready to accept blame or responsibility. He knew the gospel made sense, but he chose not to believe it.

Even though John has still (to this day) not responded in faith to the gospel, it is important to acknowledge that just because we do the hard work of sharing a believable gospel, it doesn't guarantee we will always get the hoped-for response. When we don't see an immediate response, this doesn't mean our gospel witness was in vain. Loving, listening, and speaking a believable gospel is always glorifying to God, and it can bear fruit days, months, even years later. Even rejection can be a fruit of gospel ministry, and most conversions are a process.

HOW LONG SHOULD WE WAIT TO SHARE THE GOSPEL?

Up to now, I've spend a great deal of time emphasizing the importance of sharing the gospel in the context of long-term relationships. Why? Because many people are unwilling to listen to what we have to say until we first spend time listening to them, and that usually doesn't happen in a five-minute conversation. But does this mean that we should *always* walk this long relational road before we talk about Jesus? Does a relationship always need to be formed?

Not necessarily. There are some things that are so urgent, so weighty, and so wonderful that we feel free sharing them with complete strangers! When our favorite sports team scores to win the game, we don't look around the stadium and think: "I can't tell people how happy I am about this win. I don't even know them!" We don't wait to express our

Does a relationship *always* need to be formed? Not necessarily. The truth is that when you encounter something truly wonderful, you don't limit your joy to those you know well. There are some things that are so urgent, so weighty, and so wonderful that we feel free sharing them with complete strangers!

joy; we burst out when our team wins. Or if you are at a concert and your favorite song is played, and the band is really jamming, you don't wait to sing along or comment. You join in the singing and chat it up with complete strangers. When something is truly wonderful, we don't wait to talk about it. We naturally evangelize—we share the good news with anyone who happens to be near us.

The news about Jesus certainly qualifies as good news. It's urgent, weighty, and wonderful, so wonderful that we should want to talk about it with anyone near us. Yet for some reason, it isn't always that way for us. Why? Sometimes it's because we are simply enjoying rest, perhaps taking a needed break. We may not share the gospel because we are enjoying the freedom of the gospel. However, often we aren't excited about the gospel because it's not on our mind or suffusing our actions. This is because we aren't immersed in the goodness of the gospel. We aren't enjoying the gospel, taking in its story and being mesmerized by its central character. Instead, competing stories of success, entertainment, or comfort lure us away from Jesus. We don't talk about Jesus because we aren't taken with him.

When gospel goodness hasn't worked its way down to our heart, it isn't the story that informs the way we think about life. We don't see God as the central character of our life; we still see ourselves in that role. As a result, conversations and reflections tip toward us. However, when we are soaking in the manifold beauty of Christ, the gospel doesn't seem like old hat to us. Fresh encounters with Christ have a way of spilling over into our conversations with others. We are prone to talk about the gospel when the good news is good news to us.

A HAIRCUT AND UNION WITH CHRIST

I was on my way to Birds Barbershop to get a haircut. Birds is iconically Austin—punk music, random furniture, wall art that requires 3-D glasses (which they provide), and, of course, service with an attitude. It's in the heart of Austin counterculture. Before I sit down, they offer me the typical options: a Lone Star beer (it's Texas) or a bottle of water.

My usual hairdresser wasn't in that day, but my hair was overdue for a cut. I plopped down in the barber chair to get my haircut by a new hairdresser. Risky, I know. The things we do for the gospel!

Amber was my barber that day, and after introducing myself, I asked Amber what she loved about cutting hair. We talked about her job and the challenges that come along with it. Then came that typical question: "So what do you do?"

"I'm a pastor of a church that gathers downtown, City Life Church," I replied. "Our vision is to bring life, not take life, from the city." I shared with her our sense that Christians have a terrible reputation for being indifferent to the needs of the city and why we are devoting ourselves to renewing the city socially, spiritually, and culturally. I could tell this piqued her interest. She asked me to explain what I was talking about, so I shared some examples of various things we do in the city. I explained how our City Groups serve the marginalized through feeding the homeless, hanging out with fatherless kids, and mentoring children at a local shelter. I also mentioned our nonprofit, Music for the City, which promotes the music of upcoming artists through compilation albums, festivals, and concerts. She thought that was pretty cool.

I could have stopped there. My hairdresser thinks church is cool; that's awesome — this doesn't happen every day. I could have just invited her to church, but as I sat in the chair, the Spirit prompted me to go a little further. I sensed God's love for Amber, and it pressed against my vocal chords. So at the risk of rejection, I asked Amber if she had any religious background. She told me that her grandmother had taken her to church when she was young, but that she hadn't been to a church in at least ten years. She recalled the people being nice, but she didn't see the relevance of church. It seemed so backward, out of touch with reality.

Amber isn't alone. People everywhere think the church is out of touch and irrelevant today. As a result, they fail to see any relevance in the gospel. Amber hadn't ever heard someone talk about a city-changing gospel before. So she was intrigued. As my lap was showered with hairs, we continued to talk. Sensing the haircut was coming to a close, I circled back to our discussion about our church: "You know, Amber, the reason I do all this stuff for the city isn't because I'm a great person. I'm not even a great pastor; it's because I have a great God. I've had a profound personal encounter with Jesus Christ and he has utterly changed me." Because I belong to Jesus Christ, I wanted Amber to know that the good things we were doing weren't really about us. They were about Jesus. My union with Christ prompted me to go public about the reason for my joy and my love for the city. Sometimes, sharing something wonderful shouldn't wait.

I had no relationship with Amber before I sat down in her barber chair. Yet, in the span of forty-five minutes we had a meaningful conversation about life, vocation, church, and Christ. Did I wait to share the gospel with her until she trusted me, knew my family, and had visited a church gathering? No. But the love of God compelled me (2 Corinthians 5:14). She wasn't a to-do on my evangelistic checklist. It wasn't something I felt forced to do. I wasn't recruiting for our church; I was rejoicing in the truth about my Savior and what he was doing through me.

If there's one thing many urbanites can detect, it's a lack of authenticity. Inundated by manipulative marketing, pop-up ads, and spam, we can't stand a fake. So when we share from a heart of genuine affection for Christ, it's compelling, if not convincing. We don't need to trump it up. Because I was soaking in the gospel, I spoke from a place of authentic love for Jesus. The love of Christ compelled me to ask her questions, not bombard her with doctrines. I didn't lead off with a gospel presentation; I loved her like a person. I showed genuine interest in her job, empathized with her objections regarding church, complimented her on my haircut, and at the end of our time, tipped her well.

Our conversation about Jesus wasn't forced because it came about as a direct result of questions we asked one another. There was no pitch. What I sensed in the moment was genuine awe over what God is doing, so instead of giving credit to the church or myself, I gave credit to Jesus. I shared with her that it all boiled down to Jesus, to a personal encounter with him. I talked about Jesus because I was taken with Jesus. I

We talk about what we are taken with.

wasn't witnessing to Amber; Amber was witnessing Christ in me, the hope of glory (Colossians 1:27)!

We all talk about what we are taken with. Have you ever considered what would have happened if Jesus waited to offer the thief on the cross eternal life until he had a relationship with him? What if authors, pastors, and preachers waited to tell you the good news until they had a relationship with you? There are things so wonderful they shouldn't wait to be shared.

You should know that not all my haircuts go like this! There are many days that I'm not taken with Jesus like this and, as a result, I don't ask good questions, and I don't speak up because I'm not personally experiencing Christ as wonderful. We all need fresh encounters with Jesus, opportunities for the gospel to awaken our hearts with fresh love for him. Then our evangelism will ring with authenticity. Our union with Christ gives our words incredible intimacy.

Like the other needs we've looked at, the search for intimacy isn't on the surface of everyone's story. Not everyone will resonate with a deep need for love. That's okay. God has provided a variety of ways for us to bring the truth of the gospel to bear on people's lives.

As we will see in the next chapter, sometimes what matters most to people is tolerance. Just as we have seen with our need for acceptance, hope, and intimacy, the gospel speaks to our need for tolerance as well.

KEY QUESTIONS

1. How do you know when someone is searching for intimacy? Can you spot anyone like that in your life?
2. How can you share the hope of union with Christ? Practice on your Christian friends!
3. Why does union with Christ motivate authentic witness without a relationship with someone?

chapter twelve

SEEKING TOLERANCE

Living in Austin, I am frequently asked if I believe that Jesus is the only way to God. Most people aren't into that. As we saw in chapter 4, new tolerance is part of our urban ethos. We celebrate diversity, and the more diverse the better. The problem is that many people don't see that they are inconsistent in their understanding of tolerance. They are willing to be tolerant of everyone—except those who make exclusive claims. As soon as you state a view that suggests that someone else is wrong, like saying that Jesus is the *only* way to God, it smacks of bigotry. What lies behind this pursuit of tolerance, and how does the gospel speak to this need, this craving of the human heart?

EXCLUSIVE TRUTH WITH A BUDDHIST MONK

I had just landed in Bangkok, Thailand. Part of our cultural orientation included a visit to the Temple of the Emerald Buddha before traveling upcountry to do ethnographic research among the unreached Shan-Dai peoples of Northern Thailand and Myanmar. The temple is a national icon and is considered the most sacred Buddhist temple in Thailand. It sits in a sprawling square of 234 acres, surrounded by many other structures and temples, all ornately designed, making their way upward with narrow, sky-scraping spires. As a Christian, the experience is simultaneously enthralling and heart-breaking. A mix of wonder and grief fills your heart as you take in the beauty and recognize the devotion required to build these temples and worship their false gods.

Intrigued, I began to chat with some of the temple priests. I praised the structures and inquired about their religion. My questions soon led to a philosophical discussion regarding truth. As I explained the exclusive truth claims of Christianity, the monk I was talking with, wrapped in a traditional orange sarong, tilted his shaven head and said: "A tree can be blown in many directions."

Immediately, I was struck by the difference between our Western and Eastern ways of thinking. In the West, we don't respond to logic with imagery like this. So what was the monk saying? He was suggesting that some spiritual winds blow the truth in the direction of Christianity while other winds blow the truth in the direction of Buddhism. In other words, regardless of where the tree sways, Buddhism or Christianity, it is still the tree of truth.

I'll admit. I was stumped. But not just stumped, I was intrigued. I was beginning to understand a bit of how the Eastern mind, and Buddhists in particular, think. I had studied some of this in seminary, the two philosophical streams of Buddhism, but with a Western hat on. Now I was in the East, on the inside of their culture. As a result, I could appreciate their perspective on the gospel. I was learning firsthand by sitting at the feet of this Buddhist priest.

At the same time, I also knew I needed to respond. I silently prayed and then spoke. "That's an interesting response, and it is true, the tree does sway in different directions, but the tree also has roots." I was trying to contextualize, using the image he had given me. Yes, trees do sway, but they are also rooted in one place. My point was that there are still only one set of roots. Either the gospel of Christ or the Fivefold Noble Path would support that trunk of truth; it can't be both. The tree can only bend so far or it snaps. We parted cordially with lots to think about. It had been a profitable conversation for both of us. I learned to listen and was challenged to think about how to speak the gospel in a more believable way to a tolerant Buddhist.

As you talk with people today, you are guaranteed to encounter

Respectful dialogue can go a long way in overturning bigoted impressions of Christianity.

similar questions about the tolerance of the Christian faith. Most people will not like the exclusive claims that Christianity makes. However, before scoffing at their perspective or trying to crush their worldview, we do well to ask questions, to get on the inside of their perspective and appreciate their views. Respectful dialogue can go a long way in overturning bigoted impressions of Christianity. In fact, it will open doors that would remain closed otherwise.

PLURALISM ON A BARSTOOL

Buddhism is one of the three great missionary religions. Islam is another. Let's return to my interaction with Dave and Brian in chapter 4 at the Gingerman pub. If you recall, Brian was questioning Jesus' exclusive claims. He said to me: "So what about the Muslims? I mean they're serious too. They are willing to *die* for what they believe. Are you saying that they won't go to heaven?" How do you respond to this?

I responded to Brian by saying: "Brian, I respect these people for their sincerity. They are more serious about their faith than many Christians, but just because they are sincere doesn't mean they are right. Many people are sincerely wrong about all kinds of things. There were scientists who were sincerely wrong about the earth being the center of the universe. We shouldn't mistake sincerity for truth." Brian told me that he'd have to think more about that.

I moved on from that to talk about the eternal destiny of sincere Muslims. As we talked, I encouraged him to evaluate what Jesus said about himself in John 14:6: "I am the way and the truth and the life" — not a way,

Just because people are sincere about their religious views doesn't make them right.

a truth, a life. I pointed out that those who espouse tolerance often value sincerity over truth. While the desire for sincerity is important, it's not all that matters. Jesus brought sincerity and truth together. In fact, he showed us that *real love is being sincere about the truth.* It is not just a matter of tolerating other people and their beliefs. If we sincerely care about others and are committed to truth, we will challenge their deeply held beliefs with respect.

After sketching some of the major distinctions between Islam and Christianity, I made a simple observation about the uniqueness of Christ. "In all major world religions, a religious code is devised to *work our way to God.* The problem, however, is that we can't keep all the rules and adhere to all the ways. We are imperfect. But in Christianity, God *works his way down to us.* He keeps all the rules; he makes the way. This is called grace. It is the fundamental difference between Christianity and other religions. Sincere self-sacrifice, while noble, does not make us acceptable to a holy God. Rather, we need someone who is perfect to sacrifice for our failure to honor God and to present us acceptable to him. This is what Jesus did. No other religion offers this—where God gets hurt on behalf of his people, dies, rises from the dead, and then makes them acceptable, forgiven, and righteous."

I don't remember Brian's exact response that night. We continued to talk; he continued to ask questions. I know there was some heavy head nodding and a genuine openness to what I was saying. Now, several years after that conversation, Brian is married, helps to lead worship in a local church, and is committed to the unique way of grace found in Jesus.

Christianity is unique, not because Christians are better than other people, but because Christ is better than any of us. He is a better answer to our problems. In Christianity, God dies so man can live.[1] In other religions, human beings live in the uncertain hope that they won't really die. In the gospel, God works his way down to us in Jesus to bear our load and give us his life. In most religions, man works his way up to God, bearing an unbearable load with a vague hope of afterlife.

Christ is utterly unique. He dies and lives again so that we can die and truly live. By faith, his death and resurrection becomes our death and resurrection. Jesus is the substitute sacrifice, the self-sacrifice of God to reconcile estranged, indifferent, distrusting, and even hostile sinners. This is called *redemption*. To move forward in persuasive tolerance, Brian needed to hear how the gospel was unique, unlike any other religious perspective.

God's law reveals our need for redemption, showing us that we need someone to pay the penalty for our sinful crimes. The gospel metaphor of redemption proclaims that Christ paid that penalty for us. It was a gift, an act of *grace*. With a death sentence hanging over us, Jesus stepped up to serve our sentence. He made atonement, taking on himself God's wrath and anger for our sins — despite the fact that he himself had no sin. The sinless perfection and mind-blowing grace we see in the gospel makes Jesus utterly unique, exclusively gracious, and the one and only way to be reconciled to a holy God. While others insist on works, we must insist on grace, tethered to Jesus, who extends saving mercies through his essential death in our place. To reject Jesus as the only way to the Father is to reject our only way to be forgiven and redeemed: "In

Christianity is utterly unique, not because Christians are better than other people, but because Christ is better than any of us.

him we have redemption through his blood, the forgiveness of our trespasses, according to the riches of his grace" (Ephesians 1:7).

Through the gospel metaphor of redemption, I was able to communicate the uniqueness of Christ in comparison with other religions. My goal in doing this was not to demean Islam or mock Muslim sincerity and religious fervor. In fact, I praised their sincerity, but I avoided the fallacy of the new tolerance, where everything is equally true. Instead, I honored what is honorable in Islam but focused attention on the unique and marvelous truth revealed in the gospel of Jesus Christ. Jesus granted people the dignity to believe whatever they choose to believe, yet he was clear that it was only by faith in him that they would be saved. He "intolerantly" insisted on his unique way to the Father, and he was willing to die for his conviction that his death would lead to life for sinners who trust in him.

REDEMPTIVE TOLERANCE FOR ARTISTS

One of the most sincere people I know is Ben Roberts. Ben has a sordid history with church. He describes it this way: "The church I left was a church obsessed with football, guns, Rush Limbaugh, carpet bombing the Middle East, and bad praise music. Culture was like a Thomas Kincaid painting by the dining room table. I was a sensitive soul. I loved literature, philosophy, and architecture. Every time I opened my mouth I felt like I had said something totally insane and idiotic. By the time I was a teenager I felt so out of place, I was plagued by suicidal thoughts. So I left that culture and realized there were all sorts of people like me—only they didn't go to church. They were in the bars and art studios. So screw church."

Ben was seeking tolerance and respect, where everyone has a place at the table no matter what kind of person they are. Unfortunately, many evangelical churches have a tendency to create institutional conformity that obliterates differences. As a creative person, Ben values diversity. He longed for the freedom to discuss new ideas, argue alternative views, and step outside the narrow confines of church culture. He is not alone. Many artists feel as if the church is an intolerant institution that puts different perspectives to death and creates mindless, indoctrinated drones. Some stay in the church and suffer, but many others just leave.

When Ben came to our church, he found that we were willing to bend some of the traditional religious boundaries, and he was intrigued. He began attending our Sunday gatherings regularly and participating in a City Group. We've had some great discussions about writing, art, and culture. While we don't always agree, I always walk away with a deeper appreciation for life. After a conversation with Ben, I see the world differently—often better. When Ben realized that we weren't going to try and change him, and that we would actually engage his views on art, philosophy, literature (and Metallica), he was thrown off balance. He saw, for the first time, that the church can be a place of tolerance, even a place of love. I asked him to share his thoughts on this, and he wrote:

> At City Life, I felt like I fit right in ... or I fit in as much I should ever expect to fit in. People would actually talk about books and art. They weren't mindless, tasteless Jesus zombies. They even told me a few things. I remember carefully explaining to a friend that Metallica's "Leper Messiah" is a valid artistic expression. Matt's response was like, "Duh, Metallica can express truth. Just remember: All truth is God's truth."

Ben encountered a group of loving Christians who pitched a kingdom tent for truth, not a denominational tent. What was most striking to him was the spirit of hospitality and respect, that he wasn't shunned for talking about topics like alcohol abuse. Ben encountered the hope of redemption while digging through topics like depression and abortion. There wasn't a conversionary moment that finally drew him to Christ. Instead, Ben radically reoriented to Christ over time through the influence of a persuasively tolerant *community*, one that by all appearances had nothing in common with each other.

One night, after a City Group gathering, Ben turned to his wife and commented: "These people have nothing in common except Jesus." We take that as a compliment! And if it sounds familiar, it should. Jesus once said: "By this all people will know that you are my disciples, if you have love for one another" (John 13:35). The church isn't a loose collection of religious individuals; it is a loving community united together around Jesus. When we put aside our selfishness, our fear of differences,

The church isn't a loose collection of religious individuals; it is a loving community united together around Jesus.

and our disagreements, and begin to love those who are different from us, we begin to glow with the light of Christ. Ben's community was unified, not by life stage, subculture, ethnicity, or vocation. Instead, their unifying hope in the Redeemer lit the way for them to be together.[2]

The gospel of redemption creates common ground for uncommon people. It unites us at a deep level that transcends tastes, hobbies, and pet peeves. When Jesus is central we have a basis for shared forgiveness, love, acceptance, and tolerance. When a church plugs into the gospel of redemption, the light burns so brightly that it will attract even the most unlikely of people. Even crazy artists.

KEY QUESTIONS

1. Do you know anyone who values tolerance? Try getting into a conversation with them about the difference between classical and new tolerance.
2. Ask someone about their religious beliefs without interrupting or correcting them. Just listen.
3. Why is Christianity unique among the religions?
4. How does Jesus offer redemptive tolerance? What does he tolerate at the cross?

chapter thirteen

SEEKING APPROVAL

Who doesn't want approval? We all want our mothers, fathers, heroes, and even peers to think well of us. My father is a remarkable man. He has accomplished a lot with what he's been given. Our early years were spent in a rented house, 127 Sanders St., located literally on the "wrong" side of the railroad tracks. Instead of climbing the career ladder to get us into a nicer house, my Dad started a window cleaning business so he could have a flexible schedule and maximize time with his three sons. He coached our sport teams, showed up for our school performances, and supported our personal hobbies. Dad was present. He also made sure he had individual conversations with us, deliberately learning how to love each of his three sons uniquely. We matured under the sun of our father's approval.

He was also the kind of dad that friends love. When we had friends over, he would wrestle us on the living room floor, hang out and make jokes, and show genuine interest in whatever we were into at the time. My father was also a spiritual leader in the home, teaching us to value the truth, practice integrity, and honor Christ. Mom silently modeled and prayed all of this into us. As we got older, Dad went on to become an English and literature teacher at a junior college for ten years, and then retired to start a dotcom, where he is currently the CEO. He is also an active elder, teacher, and discipler in his church.

Why all the detail about my dad? Well, for all practical purposes, I had a great father. Sure, he wasn't perfect, but he was present and even exemplary in many ways. I always sensed his love and approval. Even now that I'm older, with a family of my own, he isn't afraid to tell me how proud he is that I've used my adult years to serve Christ through writing and pastoring. It means so much to me to hear those words from him, more than anyone else—peers, mentors, or heroes. When I told him this in my late thirties, he was shocked. He figured that since flying the nest and soaring the winds of maturity, I no longer needed his approval.

The thoughts and opinions of parents matter to their children. What my dad and mom thought about me as I was growing up meant something. Their thoughts and opinions could crush or lift me in a moment. We are made for approval, and though our parents are often the first ones to give this (or withhold it from us), the truth is that we seek this approval from others all the time. Our sense of approval consciously or unconsciously affects our thoughts, choices, and actions every day. This is true of everyone, especially those whom we are praying will turn to Christ.

I met James in an intensive recovery weekend program called Discovery. I'll admit that I had no idea what I was getting myself into.

We are made for approval, and though our parents are often the first ones to give this (or withhold it from us), the truth is that we seek this approval from others all the time.

My wife asked me to go through the program, and I reluctantly agreed because I knew it meant something to her. I figured that it couldn't hurt, and I'd probably learn a few things that would help me be a better pastor. Perhaps I'd even be able to help someone in the program.

James was the first person I met while waiting to go into our first session. I was immediately drawn to him. At first glance, you'd assume we had nothing in common. He was young, dressed "gangsta," and clearly depressed. I'm a pastor, dress differently, and have some lift in my step.

When it came time to pick our "buddies" for the duration of the program, I chose James without hesitation. I wanted to be in his life. The Holy Spirit had already drawn my attention to him earlier. Being buddies meant we were tethered for the next three days. We shared meals, awkward exercises, storytelling that uncovered secrets, and moments of intense vulnerability. We ran the gamut of emotions—bitter anger to joyful weeping. As I got to know James, I learned he had been given up for adoption at an early age. I had a hard time tracking with his various guardians. Because of his early rejection and tumultuous upbringing, he had a lifelong gnawing in his heart to find and meet his biological mother. He wanted an answer to the question *why*—"Why did you give me up?" He eventually found his mother, but she could not give him the answers, attention, or approval he longed for.

After several twists and turns in his journey, including an addiction to meth and now recovery, he had grown numb. You could see the numbness in his complexion. When he stood up to share why he was in the group, he confessed: "I feel nothing. I use [drugs] to distract myself from the emptiness. I want to feel joy again, but know it's impossible." As I hung out on smoke breaks with James and worked through the intensive exercises, it became apparent that he desperately craved approval. I worked hard during our times together to model for him the kind of approval my father had shown me. I supported him, counseled him, and encouraged him. I loved James.

As we continued to work through the recovery process, James reached a crossroads. Although he had unearthed a buried pining for his mother's acceptance, he was reluctant to forgive her. Earlier he had privately told me the one thing he would *not* do was forgive his mother. I had assured him no one would force him to do anything, while simultaneously praying that he would experience the forgiveness of Christ. As he let anger go, he remarked, "I want my faith back."

Growing up, James had intermittently attended a Methodist church. Standing in front of him, I put each of my hands on his shoulders, looked him in the eyes, and said, "James, I want to tell you a story that Jesus shared." I shared with him the story of the prodigal son from Luke 15, and I told him that God the Father wasn't just standing on the porch waving his finger at him with a reprimanding scowl. "God the Father sees you, James, and he is running out to meet you right now. He is ready to throw his arms around you, give you his ring and robe, and tell you he loves you. Though you feel rejected, God is inviting you home, James. He's saying, 'Come home, James. Come home. I love you like no other person can.'"

James collapsed under the Father's love saying, "I believe," and we fell into one another's arms, where I held him for at least sixty seconds, as he sobbed uncontrollably in my chest. The promises of Scripture that I had shared with him had given birth to new hope in his heart. But even more importantly, James had finally found the home he had been searching for. He had experienced the power of the enduring, perfect approval of Christ.

We finished our time in the Discovery program, and I headed home. Less than ten days later, I learned that James died from meningitis. Yes, dead. At his funeral, I stood up in a room full of strangers to reflect on his precious life. I was able to share the good news I had personally witnessed, that James had been adopted into the Father's family. The providential intervention of God's grace in James's life is one for the history books. The timing of his enrollment in Discovery, my reluctant participation, his remarkable breakthrough and salvation in Christ all converged in one massive weekend of grace to make a slave into a son. James found his true way home.

Our hearts long for approval, and no matter how terrible or how great our family life, the approval of Mom and Dad will never be enough. Nor can the approval of a teacher, coach, friend, or spouse fill that void. At best, these relationships offer us an imperfect glimpse. What we need is the adopting love of our heavenly Father.

ADOPTION IN A KINKO'S

The gospel metaphor of adoption is moving. When we turn to Christ, adoption confers on us the undying approval of God the Father, sweeping us into his family as his very own sons and daughters. In his family we are loved, not in spite of our failures but because of them. The Father sees us stranded in our insistence that some human supply what only he can offer. Moved by compassion, he sends his Son to rescue us from idolatrous pursuits of human approval. Adoption is also personally redemptive. When we fail the Father or give him the finger, he beckons us home. All we have to do is turn around, and like the father of the prodigal son, he runs to cast his lavish embrace on us (Luke 15:20)!

To turn around, however, we have to be freed from our slavery to things that have power over us. In Galatians 4:1–7, Paul tells us that adoption results in a permanent change in status, from slave to a son. He points out that, apart from Christ, we are enslaved to the "elementary principles of the world." These principles hold power over us. In order to escape, we need to be pried out of the hands of the powers. We might be enslaved to the mastery of what a peer, parent, boss, or absolute stranger thinks about us. Alternatively, we may be enslaved to an idealistic, relational fantasy where those around us meet our every emotional need. In either case, what we long for is the approval of others instead of resting in the approval we have in Christ.

One day, I was in a Kinko's to get a copy of a book manuscript. I had just returned from a Christian conference, and I was wearing my conference T-shirt. Standing in line, I found myself gripped by fearful thoughts, suddenly embarrassed to be wearing a "Christian" T-shirt. What if the Kinko's guy reads my shirt and asks me about it? What will I say? Then, I thought about the book he was printing off. What if he reads the title, *Gospel-Centered Discipleship*? What will I say? In that moment I was filled with fear, worried what a random guy at Kinko's thought about me and not what he thought about Christ. I feared the loss of his approval—a complete stranger! How preposterous! You mean an author who writes about faith in the gospel loses faith in the gospel? Oh yes, every single day, which is why I'm so deeply moved by God's enduring approval and love. I abandon it in a moment for the slavery of human approval, but still he loves me.

Perhaps you don't struggle with approval. My brother, Luke, can strike up a conversation with anyone about anything and never seems to care what other people think. I find that amazing, because I have to work at it. While I don't want to detract from that strength, sometimes our slavery of choice is approval on steroids—applause. Instead of being hampered by people thinking less of us, we want people to think more of us. Rather than longing for someone to look down on you in approval, perhaps you just want others to look up and applaud: "He's so successful." "She's so wise!"

The search for applause is hope in hyperapproval. No matter which master we choose, the gospel frees us from the struggle or search to derive confidence from human approval. The gospel tells me that I was so sinful that Christ had to die for me, but it also says God is so gracious that he lives for me. Jesus died for our willful slavery to fleeting masters, and he lives again to bring us into devotion to a more dignifying Master. Other masters make us grovel for approval or overwork for applause, but not Christ. Instead, he is chained to death to liberate us into his life. In Christ, we hit the gospel jackpot by the grace of God. The proof of our winnings is this: we are forever *humbled* that God would adopt us into his family, yet *confident* that Christ's work is sufficient and lasting. Hope in Jesus keeps us from both prideful arrogance and from self-doubt. How? We no longer hang our worth or value on our perceived performance. Instead, we hang our worth and value on what Jesus has done for us.

Faith in the gospel produces *humble confidence*—humble because we know how undeserving we are, and confident because of God's rich devotion to us in Christ. Adoption is a change in status from slave to son or daughter that happens through the Spirit of God: "God has sent the Spirit of his Son into our hearts, crying, "Abba! Father! So you are no longer a slave, but a son, and if a son, then an heir through God" (Galatians 4:6–7). Notice that the Spirit doesn't just give us a new status—one of great value; he gives us a voice before our Father. The Spirit of the Son cries out "Abba! Father!" This word, "Abba," is an Aramaic word that most believe means "dearest Father." Some try to pick up on this meaning by addressing God as "Dad," but they miss the point. While referring to God the Father as "Dad" picks up on the certain love of God, it also detaches his love from his transcendent holiness.

The term *Abba* is uniquely used by Jesus in Scripture (Matthew 6:9; John 14:21; 20:17) and is probably the basis for his use of the word "Father." In each use, Jesus refers to his unique relationship with God the Father, often combining a sense of God's holiness with his love. For

Jesus dies for our willful slavery to fleeting masters, and he lives again to bring us into devotion to a more dignifying Master. Other masters make us grovel for approval or overwork for applause, but not Christ. Instead, he is chained to death to liberate us into his life.

example, he assures the disciples they need not be afraid, while also affirming the greatness of God when he says, "the Father is greater than I" (though Christ is no less divine, John 14:28). Jesus also frequently associates an experience of the love of God with obedience to God the Father (14:23–24, 31; 15:8–10). The Father possesses what theologian David Wells calls "the holy-love of God."[1] The picture of God the Father that emerges is one of intimacy and reverence, something Jesus knew perfectly in his relationship with the Father.[2]

With this in view, adoption is all the more striking. God draws us up into the sonship of Christ, where we too may adore the Father's holiness and enjoy his love. As a result, adoption by this Father becomes the foundation of humble confidence. We are humbled by the greatness of God and confident in his enduring love. We gain an audience with greatness. Our voice before Father God is because of the work of the Spirit and the Son. The Father listens to our fears, receives our worship, and grants us the approval our hearts long for. Were God not so great, his approval would not be so good. When we are adopted into the Father's family, we gain an unmatched and incorruptible love, superior to the love of others: "See what kind of love the Father has given to us, that we should be called children of God; and so we are" (1 John 3:1). Our appropriate response is reverence and intimacy, awe and love.

The gospel of adoption confers what we truly need—admiration of a holy God *and* enjoyment of his perfect love. This perfect blend can

The gospel of adoption confers what we truly need — admiration of a holy God *and* enjoyment of his perfect love.

be found nowhere else, and yet it is what people seek among imperfect candidates. James needed a God who was holy enough to establish the need for forgiveness and loving enough to grant it. Weighed down by his own sin and suffering, he could only experience freedom when he relinquished his demands for perfect love from his imperfect mother.

Many of us need to do the same. There is a silent pining for perfect love behind many people's aversions to God. The gospel will become believable to them when they understand the holy love of God the Father. Instead of beginning with sin or the cross, we may need to begin with the fatherhood of God. The best way to do this is to inquire about their relationship with their own parents. The inadequacy, failure, or downright horror of some parental experiences needs redeeming. Once we draw out this need in others, we gain an opportunity to share a believable gospel. We get to tell them about a God who is strong enough (holy) and weak enough (loving) to do something about their need for approval — on a cross.

KEY QUESTIONS

1. Do you know anyone like James, longing for approval? How can you show it to them?
2. How does the gospel of adoption offer more than even the best of parents or mentors?
3. What happens when we replace the gospel of adoption for the approval of others?

chapter fourteen

EVANGELISM IN COMMUNITY

None of the stories in this book could have been recorded without the vital partnership of my church. In most cases, each person who heard a gospel metaphor from me also heard the gospel and saw its power in community. This collective witness is, more often than not, how God discloses his manifold wisdom to the world (Ephesians 4:4–6). The church is God's evangelistic genius, not isolated people with evangelistic drive. In fact, people rarely come to faith from a single gospel witness. Truth be told, most conversions are the result of a process that occurs over time and involves a variety of different gospel testimonies and experiences.

Professor of evangelism Richard V. Peace writes: "Research indicates that no more than 30 percent of all conversions are punctiliar in nature. Most conversions take place over time, often with many fits and starts as one moves toward Jesus and his way. For most people conversion is a process, not an event."[1] If this is true, it would be a disservice to not share some of the community's contributions from each story. Omitting them would not only dishonor the role others have played, but also leave you with the unfortunate and inaccurate impression that successful evangelism really does hang on your lone witness. This is the opposite of what I have tried to communicate. Therefore, I'd like to circle back around to some of these stories to bring out roles played by others and lift up the importance of the local church.

The church is God's evangelistic genius, not isolated people with evangelistic drive. In fact, people rarely come to faith from a single gospel witness. Most conversions are the result of a process that occurs over time and involves a variety of different gospel testimonies and experiences.

We first met Ben in chapter 10, whose broken life of drug addiction was healed by the gospel light of new creation. Ben's introduction to Christ was the product of community. His sister-in-law picked him up when he was strung out and tried to help him get on his feet. She introduced me to Ben and accompanied me when I visited him in rehab. After Ben got out, another pastor discipled him for a season, meeting with him regularly. But perhaps his most formative experience was becoming part of a city group, a Jesus-centered community that loved him through thick and thin.

In our church, corporate witness is a critical part of how we share the gospel in the city.[2] It was with his city group that Ben discovered true, Christ-centered community. They discussed and applied Sunday sermons, shared meals (Ben often provided desserts), laughed and celebrated, served the poor, and planned his baptism party. Ben's experience taught him that he was saved into a community, not to a private relationship with Jesus. Many people played a role in guiding Ben to Christ. Several of them were particularly close. They helped him explore his doubts, encouraged his faith, and discipled him into a believable understanding of the gospel.

In chapter 12, we met Dave and Brian, who grappled with the exclusive claims of Jesus. As musicians, they rubbed shoulders with quite a few Christian artists in our city. The lead singer in their band has a powerful redemption story. I have no idea how many gospel conversations they had with fellow artists. I do know that they saw the power of the gospel through the nonprofit we started called Music for the City. As participants in Music for the City, both Dave and Brian used their art to help teach marginalized kids cello and violin, right alongside Christian artists who mentored these kids. Dave was gracious enough to invite one of our musicians into his life and studio, where they recorded a song together and spent late nights talking theology and art. Dave and Brian received the gospel in stereo, through word and deed, and eventually turned to Christ for salvation and hope. A chorus of gospel voices is stronger and more compelling than a lone voice in the wind.

Many stories are messy, incomplete, and still unfolding, like Doreen, who parted ways over the resurrection; John, who is still on his search for intimacy outside of Christ; and Steve, who is still searching for significance and has since divorced his wife. Each of these people were loved, served, and exhorted through multiple relationships, even whole communities. This should remind us that the church bears the responsibility of evangelism but not the power of conversion. I could go on and on, filling out the picture with various people who have contributed in gospel witness to the stories I have told. It takes a church. Unfortunately, we often reduce the mission to "personal evangelism," effectively

The church bears the responsibility of evangelism but not the power of conversion.

cutting people off from God's work in and through a community. In fact, Jesus insisted that the world would know we are his followers by our love for one another (John 13:35). We need to think more deeply and practice more consistently a communal form of evangelism.

COMMUNAL VERSUS PERSONAL EVANGELISM

Evangelism is not just an individual affair. In the West, individualistic thinking has contaminated just about every aspect of Christianity. But biblically, evangelism is more of a community project.

The new community Jesus formed does not exist for itself, but for the world (Mark 16:15; Acts 1:8). And one of the primary goals of the unity that Jesus prayed for among his disciples (and all subsequent Christians) was unity for mission: "That they may be one, even as we are one ... As you sent me into the world, so I have sent them into the world" (John 17:11, 18). Jesus saves and then sends us *as a community*.

It is surprising to notice how few evangelistic commands we actually find in Paul's letters to the churches. Rarely do we find Paul telling individual Christians to go out and tell others about Jesus. Instead, we find more emphasis on communal life centered around the person of Jesus in the life of the Spirit. This communal life is a corporate witness to the risen Lord and is used by God to attract the attention of those who are not part of his church.

Author and professor John Dickson has argued that Paul expected the churches to support the apostles, prophets, and evangelists in their mission by participating in larger activities of mission.[3] In the Pauline letters, these include prayer, financial aid, mixing in society, gospel-adorning behavior, showing and telling the truth, public worship, as well as the usual ad hoc conversations with outsiders. Dickson draws a distinction between "proclaiming the gospel" (evangelism) and "promoting the gospel" (other activities that draw people to Christ). He believes that the church should be involved in gospel promotion, an equally worthy responsibility of the church in spreading the good news. This concept of promoting the gospel widens our scope of activities that spread the gospel message.

This emphasis on gospel promotion is not intended to minimize the ongoing importance of evangelism — that is, the clear, verbal proclamation of the gospel. In fact, both promotion and proclamation are important for effective witness. However, if persistent gospel promotion occurs without any proclamation, people are left to make up their own versions of the gospel. These conclusions will inevitably include crediting zealous individuals and noble nonprofits for their ministry instead of crediting *God* for his mercy. As a result, our endeavors may result in promoting human goodwill or nonprofit causes, not the person of Christ and his world-renewing gospel. I do not say this to suggest

It is surprising how few evangelistic commands we find in Paul's letters. Rarely do we find Paul telling individual Christians to go out and tell others about Jesus.

that every act of mercy must be accompanied by gospel proclamation. Rather, I am drawing attention to the corporate witness of the church that includes both proclamation and promotion *of the gospel*. Both must be kept together in the church.

THE MISSIONAL FAMILY

In the Gospels, we observe disciples living in community. They did not individually attend classes in which Jesus was their teacher. Instead, the disciples followed Jesus *together*. They formed a community around their Messiah. Why? They were connected to one another because they were profoundly connected in Christ. As a result, they shared just about everything: meals, prayers, evangelism, sermons, lessons with the Master, feeding the poor, communion, persecution, and the promises of God. Jesus didn't just "make disciples"; he made a new family: "And looking about at those who sat around him, he said, 'Here are my mother and my brothers!'" (Mark 3:34). Jesus drew people to himself *and* to one another. Just as he and the Father are one, he makes us into people who are one, united together (John 17:11).

Church is a necessary aspect of belonging to Christ, of being "in Christ." The Head has a Body. The Cornerstone is part of a Temple. The Vine has Branches. We are not just converted once, to Christ; we are converted three times—to Christ, to the church, and to mission.[4] To be sure, Christ alone is Lord. Our conversions to the church and to mission flow out of this fundamental union, but if Christ is your Lord, these will necessarily follow. You will belong to his family and join his mission.

New Testament scholar Joseph Hellerman states this truth well: "We do not find an unchurched Christian in the New Testament ... a person was not saved for the sole purpose of enjoying a personal relationship with God ... a person is saved *to community*."[5] If you are not meaningfully connected to other disciples, you haven't embraced the implications of your union with Christ. You haven't fully realized the meaning of your adoption. Instead, you've bought into the false gospel of individualism.

"We do not find an unchurched Christian in the New Testament ... a person was not saved for the sole purpose of enjoying a personal relationship with God ... a person is saved *to community*." — Joseph Hellerman

Perhaps you've come to believe that you have been saved into a personal relationship instead of a family of relationships united in Christ. In Christ, God is the Father of a *family* and we belong to one another. Since we share the same spiritual blood, we should act like a family. A healthy family shares life, possessions, meals, money, failures, successes, and hardships. A spiritual family shares forgiveness, grace, hope, truth, love, and most of all — Jesus. This kind of redemptive family sticks out as a gospel witness in the world

Applying the gospel in the ways we've discussed in this book is a communal endeavor. We *need* one another. Have you ever found it difficult to believe the truth or obey King Jesus in some area? It is possible to know the truth without believing the truth, especially when you are trying to go it alone. We need other people, and specifically those in the church, to help us believe and obey the truth. This is why there are so many exhortations to be a "truth and grace" community in the

New Testament. Being a gospel-fluent people is not just a matter of evangelism; it affects our discipleship — our day-to-day life as followers of Jesus.

The gospel is good news for both non-Christians *and* Christians. Steve Timmis writes: "If you find it hard to talk about Jesus with Christians, then how do you expect to talk about him with unbelievers? As you get more in the habit of talking about Jesus in the everyday with Christians, you may find it easier to talk about him with unbelievers."[6] So the place to practice applying the gospel metaphors is with other Christians. Begin by listening to others, looking for opportunities to speak the hope of a gospel metaphor into a fellow believer's life. The more deeply we apply these metaphors within the church, the more integrity we will have in our gospel witness to non-Christians. We will gain opportunities to "share the gospel with ourselves out loud."

THE ROLE OF HOSPITALITY

If the church is to both proclaim *and* promote the gospel, what does our evangelism look like as a community? Michael Green notes: "One of the important methods of spreading the gospel in antiquity was the home."[7] Homes were the base for gospel ministry. Jason used his home in Thessalonica, Titus Justus in Corinth, Philip in Caesarea, and Lydia in Philippi (Acts 17:5; 18:7; 21:8; 1 Corinthians 16:9). If homes where families lived and friends visited were the key context for evangelism, then hospitality could make or break a church's witness. Biblical hospitality involved more than having a spotless home for your friends and neighbors. It was an open door, a place of welcome to the rich and the poor, the lost and the saved, the easy and the demanding, friends and strangers.

A chorus of gospel voices is much stronger than a lone evangelistic voice.

My wife exudes hospitality. We have about fifty people a week in our home and host parties on a monthly basis. Robie goes out of her way to engage non-Christians, make conversation with newcomers, and generate a joyful atmosphere for all. She creates a context where Christian and non-Christian alike can have a good time (and lots of gospel conversations and community development occur). We've been in a new neighborhood for about a year and have had quite a few neighbors over. Thanks to the welcoming, loving home my wife has created (and our great kids), we are a lightning rod home for children under ten. Like a swarm of flies, they rush in and out, creating havoc and enjoying grace. It's a real bonus for their parents—free babysitting!

Through these open doors and the hospitality of my wife, I've gotten to know Buddhists, secularists, agnostics, and atheists—all *in community*. We mix up these get-togethers with Christians and non-Christians, and our neighbors regularly comment on how much they enjoy our church friends. Many of these have played a role in the evangelistic stories I have shared. So you see, evangelism is a community project. The church is God's missionary genius for the world. The more we invite non-Christians into our community and go into their communities, the more diverse and distinct our witness will become. A chorus of gospel voices is much stronger than a lone witness in the wind.

KEY QUESTIONS

1. Why is "personal evangelism" insufficient?
2. What advantages do we gain in communal evangelism? List them out and discuss with a friend.
3. What is the difference between gospel promotion and proclamation?
4. How can you share the gospel with yourself out loud? Why should you even consider it?
5. Since biblical hospitality is integral to evangelism, how could you take a next step in being hospitable?

SPIRIT-LED WITNESS

While testifying to the gospel is both a personal and communal privilege, we lack the power to convince anyone that Jesus Christ is Lord. We cannot reason, love, or serve people into Christ. Where, then, does the power to save come from?

POWER TO SAVE

Paul reminds us the gospel "is the power of God for salvation to everyone who believes" (Romans 1:16). How is the gospel powerful enough to save? Because the gospel announces God's potent saving commitment to those who respond in faith (1:17). The gospel is powerful because it is effectual, and it is effectual because it is *the true word about the world*. It narrates an honest account, with no spin, about us, God, and the world. Since it is true, it works. It hits the mark every time, without fail. However, its power isn't merely in its truthfulness. Gospel truth is potent because it is the truth *spoken by an omnipotent Person*. Well, three persons, to be accurate. The electing speech of Father, the saving word of the Son, and regenerating breath of the Holy Spirit work irrevocably together to effectually save sinners. God never loses anyone because he lacks no power to save; "no purpose of [his] can be thwarted" (Job 42:2).

The Holy Spirit is the third person of the Trinity, and he applies Christ's saving work to make us new creatures. Returning to Romans 1, Paul tells us the gospel is about the incarnate Son of David, who died and rose from the dead *according to the power of the Holy Spirit* (Romans 1:3–4). Just as the life-giving power of the Spirit raised Jesus from the dead, so also he imparts resurrection life to those who believe in Jesus. My point in highlighting the Spirit's work is to show that he applies the life-giving Word to make hearts alive to Christ. The power of the gospel leaves the mouth of the Father, travels through the Word of the Son, and imparts new life through the Spirit. The Trinity works together to ensure that all who are called respond to God's stunning offer in Christ. In short, the gospel is the power of *God* for salvation.

Therefore, whenever you're sharing the gospel or praying for the salvation of others, you should be comforted that God possesses all the power to save. In fact, this truth should relieve you of pressure evangelism and release you into Spirit-led evangelism. The Spirit will prompt you to share with others when and if you are walking in step

The gospel is powerful because it is effectual, and it is effectual because it is *the true word about the world*. It narrates an honest account, with no spin, about us, God, and the world.

Whenever you're sharing the gospel or praying for the salvation of others, you should be comforted that God possesses all the power to save.

with him. This doesn't have to be showy. It can be a simple thought or a deep spiritual impression. The Spirit may bring a friend's name to mind, urge you to invite a neighbor over for dinner, or compel you to share the gospel on the spot with someone. Regardless, take great hope in the promise that God works powerfully to save those whom he has called.

PESTERING PROVIDENCE

In addition to our witness, the Holy Spirit responds to our prayers. We are invited, even commanded, to pray "in the Spirit" at all times, particularly for openings to proclaim the gospel (Ephesians 6:18–20; Colossians 4:2–6). Like the widow who pestered the unjust judge, we should pepper God with prayers for the salvation of our family, friends, coworkers, and unmet, unreached peoples of the world. Jesus calls us to pray to the Lord of the harvest so that the bounty of his efficacious Word is brought forth. This is such a rich reward in itself, praying for people to be saved from sin and made into new creatures, and then to see the Lord do it. An evangelizing church is a praying church. The church that evangelizes has to pray because it knows evangelism is ineffective apart from the powerful work of the Spirit, who responds both to our prayers and to God's will.[1]

EVANGELISM IS WAR

We must also remember that evangelism is war. When we pray, speak, and act for the salvation of others, the devil doesn't take it kindly. He is a roaring lion who seeks to devour, an evil parent who would keep the sons of disobedience locked away in cellars of sin, shame, and unbelief. Evangelism is war. It is boldly encroaching on the enemy's territory, arousing a lion, and we should expect his fierce response. Satan will discourage you in your efforts, distract you in your prayers, and even buffet you with sufferings. Often he strikes to create discord in the church, to distract our attention from the mission of God. But don't be dismayed. God's saving Word is a peace-making Word and greater than the little roar of the lion. One little Word shall fell him. His defeat is as sure as the cross is true.

Christ has risen in victorious triumph over sin, death, and evil to make all things new, even us. His saving power is on display for heav-

Evangelism is war. It is boldly encroaching on the enemy's territory, arousing a lion, and we should expect his fierce response. Satan will discourage you in your efforts, distract you in your prayers, and even buffet you with sufferings.

enly rulers and authorities (Ephesians 3:10), where God shows off his power and shames the devil. This means that evangelism isn't ultimately about our converts, our methods, our disciples, our community, or even our church or ministry. There is a cosmic stage set, and the gospel is on display through the church to shame evil powers and stun angels into giving *God* all glory. Gospel witness isn't just a matter of pragmatism (doing it because it is effective); it's a matter of worship (doing it for God's fame). There is no need to count converts for our significance, but there is every reason to count on Christ and his significant, eternal, saving work for sinners.

In conclusion, we should take heart that the Spirit works in power, gives us promptings, and answers prayers in order to apply the word of our witness to bring about new creation to the glory of God.

GOOD NEWS FOR ALL

People aren't interested in a sound-bite gospel. They don't find a preachy, impersonal, intolerant, or shallow message believable. But the true gospel is so much more. In general, people want to know why they should believe what you are saying. The first place they often look is your life. Are you personally gripped by the message of grace? Or is your life defined by a search for security through possessions and money? Do you trust the Lord for the peace that passes understanding, or do you moan about the anxieties of family and work? Does your character reflect the sacrifice and beauty of Christ or the values of consumer society? Do you tower over others in pride, cower from them in fear, or possess a humble confidence that arises from your deep security in Christ? We all need re-evangelization through the various metaphors of the gospel.

The second place people look to discover if the gospel is worth believing is in our words. Much of the evangelism of the past fifty years offered a sound bite, something easily screened, distrusted, and dismissed. In order for people to see something of substance in our words, our gospel communication needs personal nuance and cultural discernment. How does the person and work of Jesus intersect with the longings, hurts, and idolatries of those around us? What do they hear when we speak? Do they ever hear about your own, ongoing personal need for Christ? Or are you recycling dusty doctrines? How has Jesus affected your life? How has the gospel changed your relationships? How has it influenced the way you live? Your marriage? Your parenting? Your work?

The gospel is such good news for all of us! It gives us authentic motives, with an eternal and diverse message about Jesus that can be communicated in a variety of methods — through gospel metaphors that speak to the different needs of the human heart. These timeless metaphors communicate various aspects of God's saving grace to people in real space and time. They communicate across cultures and generations. As we listen to others' stories, we can learn to utilize the rich range of images God has given us to speak a believable word of hope to lost and broken people.

God has invited us to join him in communicating his grace to all peoples before he returns in righteous judgment (Matthew 24:14). But how are they to believe in him of whom they have never heard? And how are they to hear without someone preaching to them? (Romans 10:14 – 15). God has sent us on his grand mission. You carry an effectual gospel and are the most effective missionary to the people you live,

God has provided a diversity of choice metaphors that culminate in otherworldly power to bring sinners into heart-thrilling union with Christ.

work, and play with. You need not fear what they think, though Satan would love for you to cower in fear. Don't fret about the disapproval of man because you have the enduring approval of God in Christ.

You do not need the power of coercion or right answers because the power for salvation does not rest in you but in the gospel itself: "For I am not ashamed of the gospel, for it is the power of God for salvation to everyone who believes" (Romans 1:16). The power of *God*. He's got this. You just get to be in on it, and he's provided a diversity of choice metaphors that culminate in otherworldly power to bring sinners into heart-thrilling union with Christ. Tell people why Jesus is good news and trust the Lord with the rest. Pray, love, listen, speak, and watch God work, setting apart the Lord Christ in your heart. Then you will have given a believable word, an authentic answer for the hope within you.

NOTES

PREFACE

1. Stephen Furtick's church, Elevate, intentionally plants already baptized Christians in the crowd, asking them to come down to the front as if they are going to get baptized in order to stimulate people who are on the fence of belief, creating a tipping point of social response to come forward for baptism. These "plants" are instructed to "move intentionally through the highest visibility areas and the longest walk." See the *Spontaneous Baptism How-To-Guide*, which you can access through www.sunstandstill.org/baptismkit (accessed May 2, 2014).

2. One such example comes from the Harvest Crusades of evangelist Greg Laurie: "Greg Laurie's staff estimates that 16,000 conversions occurred at Harvest Christian Fellowship in the five-year period from 1986 to 1991.… Perhaps only 10 percent of these decisions resulted in long-term changes in personal behavior." Donald Miller, *Reinventing American Protestantism: Christianity in the New Millennium* (Berkeley: University of California Press, 1997), 171–72, cited in Richard Peace, "Conflicting Understandings of Christian Conversion: A Missiological Challenge," *International Bulletin of Missionary Research* 28 no.1 (January 2004): 8.

3. To appreciate the complexity of this communication gap, see

Charles H. Kraft, "God, Human Beings, Culture and the Cross-Cultural Communication of the Gospel," in *Culture, Communication, and Christianity: A Selection of Writings by Charles H. Kraft* (Pasadena, CA: William Carey Library, 2002), 19–43.

CHAPTER 1: WHY PEOPLE FIND THE GOSPEL UNBELIEVABLE

1. Joshua Long, *Weird City: Sense of Place and Creative Resistance in Austin, Texas* (Austin: University of Texas Press, 2010).
2. Richard Florida, *The Rise of the Creative Class* (New York: Basic Books, 2002), 355.
3. Ed Stetzer, "Greater Austin Church Survey," conducted by Lifeway Research, 2010. The survey technically reported the percentage indicating no belief in Jesus Christ as Savior in the city center, where our church gathers.
4. Penn Jillette on YouTube: www.youtube.com/watch?v=owZc3Xq8 obk&feature=player_embedded.
5. Vampire Weekend, "Unbelievers," from the CD *Modern Vampires of the City.* Full lyrics available at: www.azlyrics.com/lyrics/ vampireweekend/unbelievers.html.
6. David Bosch, "Evangelism: Theological Currents and Cross-Currents Today," in *The Study of Evangelism: Exploring a Missional Practice of the Church* (ed. Paul W. Chilcote and Laceye C. Warner; Grand Rapids: Eerdmans, 2008), 9.
7. Evangelism Explosion has trained a whole generation to ask the "Kennedy Questions." These questions begin by asking someone, "If you died tonight, do you know if you would go to heaven?" This begins evangelism off on the wrong foot. It baits people with heaven, not Christ. The second question is, "What would you say to God to let you into his heaven?" This question is oriented toward getting the right answer, not engaging a heart of unbelief. Good evangelism will engage both the head and the heart. Perhaps a better initial question would be, "Do you find Christianity appealing; why or why not?"

8. See the survey "Is Evangelism Going Out of Style?" by Barna Group: https://www.barna.org/barna-update/faith-spirituality/648-is-evangelism-going-out-of-style#.U2PtX1TD-Uk.

CHAPTER 2: IMPERSONAL WITNESS: RELATIONSHIPS, WORK, AND FAITH

1. Robert Putnam, *Bowling Alone: The Collapse and Revival of American Community* (New York: Simon & Schuster, 2000), 61, 98.
2. Sherry Turkle, *Alone Together: Why We Expect More from Technology and Less from Each Other* (New York: Basic Books, 2012), 309.
3. Sociologists determine the strength of relationships based on a distinction between strong and weak social ties. Family and close friends constitute strong social ties, whereas acquaintances are weak ties.
4. Robert Putnam and Lewis M. Feldstein, *Better Together: Restoring the American Community* (New York: Simon and Schuster, 2003), 9 (emphasis added).
5. My reflections here have been influenced by Jerram Barrs' fine book, *Learning Evangelism from Jesus* (Wheaton, IL: Crossway, 2009), 69–80.
6. While I realize some argue that Jesus was not a carpenter, the illustration still stands.
7. Dorothy Sayers, *Creed or Chaos: Why Christians Must Choose Either Dogma or Disaster (Or, Why It Really Does Matter What You Believe)* (Manchester, NH: Sophia Institute, 1995), 70.
8. Timothy Keller, *Every Good Endeavor: Connecting Your Work to God's Work* (New York: Dutton, 2012), 76–79.
9. These are evangelistic tools designed to help lead someone to faith in Christ. The Roman Road uses various verses in Paul's letter to the Romans to chart a course from sin to salvation. The other two resources were created by Campus Crusade for Christ or Cru (The Four Spiritual Laws) and Matthias Media (Two Ways to Live).

10. Alister McGrath, *C. S. Lewis—A Life: Eccentric Genius, Reluctant Prophet* (Cambridge, UK: Tyndale House, 2013), 255.

11. Ibid, 263.

12. Barrs, *Learning Evangelism from Jesus*, 61.

13. Michael Frost, *The Road to Missional: Journey to the Center of the Church* (Grand Rapids: Baker, 2011), 41–62.

14. Hugh Halter, *Sacrilege: Following the Unorthodox Ways of Jesus* (Grand Rapids: Baker, 2011), 112. He challenges the reader to undergo this experiment. Of course, this isn't a strict rule; we should always follow the Holy Spirit's promptings.

15. See Jerram Barrs, "Francis Schaeffer: The Man and His Message," *Reformation* 21 (November 2006): 14–15. The entire last part of this book specifically addresses "what we should say" in order to communicate a more believable gospel. I put that off because I believe it is incredibly important to consider "who we are" and how we relate first.

CHAPTER 3: PREACHY WITNESS: SELF-RIGHTEOUS PROSELYTIZING

1. The idea of missional holiness is explained in Alan Hirsch, *Untamed: Reactivating a Missional Form of Discipleship* (Grand Rapids: Baker, 2010), 45–46.

2. Not all theologians make this semantic distinction. For example, in his book *The Ethics of Evangelism* (Downers Grove, IL: InterVarsity Press, 2011), Elmer Thiessen makes an extensive philosophical case for the goodness of proselytizing and persuasion. However, in the course of his argument, he does make a distinction between moral and immoral proselytizing. His "immoral proselytizing" is roughly synonymous with my description of proselytizing, whereas his "moral proselytizing" is what I would prefer to call evangelism.

3. See http://en.radiovaticana.va/news/2013/05/08/pope_francis_at_wednesday_mass:_build_bridges._not_walls/en1-690203.

4. Harvey Cox, *The Future of Faith* (New York: HarperCollins, 2009), 3.
5. For a response to this important question, see Jonathan K. Dodson and Brad Watson, *Raised? Finding Jesus by Doubting the Resurrection* (Grand Rapids: Zondervan, 2014).
6. See the clarifying article by Glenn T. Stanton, "Fact Checker: Misquoting St. Francis of Assisi," http://thegospelcoalition.org/blogs/tgc/2012/07/11/factchecker-misquoting-francis-of-assisi/
7. I continue Steve's story, and my response, in chapter 9.

CHAPTER 4: INTOLERANT WITNESS: NAVIGATING PLURALISM

1. The claim that Jesus traveled to India during the so-called "lost years" (between ages 12 and 30) is widely recognized as a fable and holds no academic merit. Wilhelm Schneemelcher writes: "The fantasies about Jesus in India were also soon recognized as pure invention. It may be added down to today that nobody has had a glimpse of the [supposed Tibetan] manuscripts with the alleged narratives about Jesus" (*New Testament Apocrypha*; vol. 1: *Gospels and Related Writings* [rev. ed.; Louisville, KY: Westminster John Knox; 1990], 84).
2. I continue this story, and my response, in chapter 12.
3. www.carseyinstitute.unh.edu/publications/Report_Immigration.pdf.
4. D. A. Carson, *The Intolerance of Tolerance* (Grand Rapids: Eerdmans, 2012), 3.
5. Ibid, 5.
6. Michael Green, *Evangelism in the Early Church* (Grand Rapids: Eerdmans, 2003), 21.
7. Jon L. Berquist, "Resistance and Accommodation in the Persian Empire, in *In the Shadow of Empire: Reclaiming the Bible as a History of Faithful Resistance* (Richard Horsley, ed.; Louisville: Westminster John Knox, 2008), 45.
8. Peter Leithart, *Babel and the Beast: America and Empires in Biblical Perspective* (Eugene, OR: Wipf & Stock, 2012).

9. Academic religious pluralism does not assume all religions lead to the same God, advocating mutually enriching interreligious dialogue. However, this is not popular practice. Therefore, we will address the relativistic, religious pluralism that is frequently encountered in ordinary conversations.

10. This point is made by Dr. Timothy Tennent in his book *Christianity at the Religious Round Table: Evangelicalism in Conversation with Hinduism, Buddhism, and Islam* (Grand Rapids: Baker, 2002).

11. Stephen Prothero, *God Is Not One: The Eight Rival Religions That Run the World* (New York: HarperOne, 2011), 3.

12. Ibid.

13. This article was brought to my attention by Jeffrey Burton Russell, *Exposing Myths about Christianity* (Downers Grove, IL: InterVarsity Press, 2012), 54. The full quote is taken from Chawkat Moucarry, "A Lifelong Journey with Islam," *Christianity Today* (March 2010): www.christianitytoday.com/ct/2010/march/index.html?start=3 (accessed April 8, 2014).

14. See full quote in chapter 1.

15. Paul Weston, ed., *Lesslie Newbigin, Missionary Theologian: A Reader* (Grand Rapids: Eerdmans, 2006), 175.

16. For a good example of this, see the work of Bob Roberts Jr. in the Global Faith Forum at www.globalfaithforum.org.

CHAPTER 5: UNINFORMED WITNESS: THINKING SECURELY

1. I share how to answer this first question in the next chapter and have answered the second question here: www.gospelcentered discipleship.com what-to-say-when-someone-says-the-bible-has-errors/.

2. Here are several books that provide a good rationale for Christian faith from simpler to more complex: C. S. Lewis, *Mere Christianity* (rev. ed.; San Francisco: HarperSanFrancisco, 2009); N. T. Wright, *Simply Christian* (Grand Rapids: Zondervan, 2010); Rebecca Pippert, *Hope Has Its Reasons: The Search to Satisfy Our Deepest Long-*

ings (Downers Grove, IL: InterVarsity Press, 2001); Timothy Keller, *The Reason for God: Belief in an Age of Skepticism* (New York: Riverhead Books, 2009). For a more comprehensive volume on a range of apologetic issues see Peter Kreeft, *Handbook of Christian Apologetics* (Downers Grove, IL: InterVarsity Press, 2005).

3. Green, *Evangelism in the Early Church*, 18.

4. This list includes a mix of evidential and presuppositional apologists. *Evidential apologetics* is primarily a reasoned defense of Christian faith based on evidence or logical argumentation. *Presuppositional apologetics* relies primarily on the truth claims within the Bible, presupposing the regenerative power of the gospel. Evidential apologetics is particularly appealing to modernists who seek the facts or evidences for faith. Presuppositional apologetics is not restricted to a cultural mind-set, but it is helpful for postmoderns, particularly when explaining the narrative appeal of Christianity. In my experience, even postmodern urbanites have modern questions about the trustworthiness of Christianity. Therefore, there is a place for both approaches. However, we must be careful to not put our faith in apologetics but in the power of the Spirit to awaken hearts to the truth and beauty of Christ crucified and risen.

5. See the evangelistic study by Tim Chester and Steve Timmis, *The World We All Want* (Epsom, Surrey, UK: The GoodBook Company, 2011). See also *The Story of God* material by Some Communities, www.gcmcollectiv.org/resources/.

6. Worldview Christianity, while helpful and true, is not enough to change the human heart. The reason for this is that our problem is not, essentially, a rational problem. The primary cause of discord with Christianity is with Christ. Since we are fundamentally creatures of desire and fail to desire Christ, a reasonable explanation of the Christian worldview is not enough to save anyone. Instead, the heart has to be captured by a greater longing for what is supremely good and beautiful, namely, Christ. We have to exchange our worship, and reason may in fact be the god that has to be exchanged. For more on the critique of worldview, see the discussion in James

K. A. Smith, *Imagining the Kingdom: How Worship Works* (Grand Rapids: Baker, 2013), 11–16.

7. Ken Myers, *All God's Children and Blue Suede Shoes: Christians and Popular Culture* (Wheaton, IL: Crossway, 1989), v.

8. Ross Douthat, *Bad Religion: How We Became a Nation of Heretics* (New York: Free Press, 2012).

9. Mark Driscoll, *A Call to Resurgence: Will Christianity Have a Funeral or a Future?* (Carol Stream, IL: Tyndale, 2013).

CHAPTER 6: CLARITY: GAINING A FRESH VISION OF THE GOSPEL

1. Don DeLillo, *White Noise* (New York : Penguin, 2009), 188–89.

2. Tweet @BurkParsons.

3. I am indebted to Timothy Keller for this way of looking at the gospel. See Keller, *Center Church* (Grand Rapids: Zondervan, 2013), 29–38. This is based on John Frame's *The Doctrine of the Knowledge of God* (Phillipsburg, NJ: Presbyterian and Reformed, 1987), 75–77. Frame establishes an epistemology based on normative, existential, and situational ways of knowing. The historical, personal, and cosmic dimensions correspond with each of these.

4. Some have posited a "gospel of the kingdom" and "gospel of salvation," which in effect creates a two-gospel paradigm. However, this is poor interpretation. D. A. Carson notes that the gospel of the kingdom, which Jesus preached, was at the same time being fulfilled on his way to complete the Gospel Story. The kingdom announced by Jesus was only possible because of where Jesus is headed in the Gospels, namely, to the cross and resurrection. Therefore, there can be only one gospel but with different foci or what I describe here as dimensions. See D. A. Carson, "What Is the Gospel? — Revisited," in *For the Fame of God's Name: Essays in Honor of John Piper* (ed. Sam Storms and Justin Taylor; Wheaton, IL: Crossway, 2010), 149–70.

5. Charles H. H. Scobie, *The Ways of Our God: An Approach to Biblical Theology* (Grand Rapids: Eerdmans, 2009), 48.

6. I address this experience of gospel-centered, Spirit-empowered change in *Gospel-Centered Discipleship* (Wheaton, IL: Crossway, 2012).
7. J. R. R. Tolkien, *The Fellowship of the Ring* (New York: Houghton Mifflin Harcourt, 1961), 361.
8. Scot McKnight, *The King Jesus Gospel: The Original Good News Revisited* (Grand Rapids: Zondervan, 2011), loc. 28–29 in Kindle book. While I think McKnight exposes contemporary shortfalls in evangelical understandings of the gospel, using the term "soterian" to refer to the personal dimension of the gospel may not be the best word. Since God's soteriological (or saving) plan is both for the elect and the world, reducing the term "soterian" to personal salvation obscures God's larger saving agenda in the world. This, of course, is not McKnight's point. Rather, he advocates for a more Israel-incorporating, creation-focused gospel that does better justice to the whole biblical story. I couldn't agree with him more on the importance of this point, which is precisely why I believe we need to use cosmic and personal, narrative and "propositional" forms of gospel communication. This book, unfortunately, had to be largely restricted to the personal dimension of the gospel. Nevertheless, my point is that we must labor to understand a person, community, and culture in order to know which form of the gospel will communicate to them in a meaningful way. After listening and observing well, we will gain discernment on how to walk wisely with outsiders in order to respond to each person with gospel-appropriate speech.

CHAPTER 7: DIVERSITY: HANDLING THE GOSPEL IN ITS DIFFERENT FORMS

1. Gospel proclamation can occur in all kinds of ways. The New Testament uses a range of words for gospel communication — preaching, teaching, conversing, speaking, counseling.
2. There are certainly many examples of open air preaching in the New Testament as a valid form of gospel communication. However, preaching is not the focus of this book.

3. See the book by Jerram Barrs on the ministry of Jesus called *Learning Evangelism from Jesus.*
4. By focusing on this approach to evangelism I in no way am maligning other valid methodologies. Jesus and Paul certainly employed other methods to communicate the gospel. Michael Green lists several methodologies employed by the early church: public evangelism, household evangelism, personal evangelism, and literary evangelism, to which we can now add electronic evangelism (*Evangelism in the Early Church*, 300–55).
5. While there are certainly more, these are the main ones. Redemption contains a subset of gospel metaphors including: atonement, reconciliation, propitiation, and expiation.
6. Ephesians 1 announces the outpouring of God's eschatological blessings on the church through the specific, yet connected gospel metaphors of: adoption (1:5), redemption (1:7), union with Christ (1:1–14), and new creation through the Spirit (1:11, 14).
7. While justification is unique in its gospel contribution, Paul shows how it relates to other gospel metaphors. For instance, in Galatians the doctrine of *justification* leads to our incorporation in the family of Abraham through the metaphor of *adoption*. This adoption happens through our *redemption* in Christ, which in turn makes us heirs of the kingdom of God, his *new creation* (Galatians 3–4).
8. Each gospel metaphor has a bigger application to the cosmos, indicating that belief in the gospel obtains a future we all want, a renewed heaven and earth. Reflecting on new creation, Jesus speaks of the *regeneration* of the world (Matthew 19:28). In terms of *justification*, Peter describes "new heavens and a new earth" where everything is "put to rights" or where righteous dwells (2 Peter 3:13). The *adoption* of the sons of God is a trigger for the healing of all creation (Romans 8:18–25). Finally, the whole world is *reconciled* to God by the blood of Jesus' cross (Colossians 1:20). Although beyond the scope of this book, the cosmic dimension of the gospel is of tremendous value in evangelism.

CHAPTER 8: FLUENCY: SPEAKING THE GOSPEL IN CULTURAL KEY

1. Green, *Evangelism in the Early Church*, 18.
2. Timothy Tennent, *Invitation to World Missions: A Trinitarian Missiology for the Twenty-First Century* (Grand Rapids: Kregel, 2010), Kindle book, loc. 124. Tennent describes the collapse of Christendom as one of seven megatrends that are shaping twenty-first-century missions. Here are the six other megatrends:
   1. The rise of postmodernism
   2. The collapse of the "West-Reaches-the-Rest" paradigm
   3. The challenging face of global Christianity
   4. The emergence of a fourth branch of Christianity
   5. Globalization
   6. A deeper ecumenism
3. To be fair, the URL pointed to a site where the gospel was explained. However, most offended Austinites would be unlikely to go to the website. Moreover, this evangelistic approach begins with depravity, not grace. Jesus often did the opposite, beginning with one's good longings for life, kingdom citizenship, and so on. More on this below.
4. I am borrowing the term "gospel fluency" from my friend Jeff Vanderstelt. He emphasizes knowing the gospel so well that we are able to apply it in many situations in order to "speak the truth in love" to Christians. I am extending the metaphor to include thoughtful, evangelistic gospel communication. Given the need for contextualization, fluency is a helpful term. When we become fluent in another language, we take the time to learn different cultural symbols and grammar in order to communicate well. Similarly, Christians should know not only the gospel, but also their cultural grammar, so that they are adept at communicating it in various cultural keys for their hearers to understand.

CHAPTER 9: SEEKING ACCEPTANCE

1. I am continuing Steve's story from chapter one.
2. Tim Chester, *You Can Change* (Nottingham, UK: Inter-Varsity Press, 2008), 27–29.

CHAPTER 11: SEEKING INTIMACY

1. Ethan Watters, *Urban Tribes: A Generation Redefines Friendship, Family, and Commitment* (New York: Bloomsbury, 2003), 1.

CHAPTER 12: SEEKING TOLERANCE

1. I realize that, in a sense, the notion that God died is untrue. Jesus clearly claimed to be divine, but was also human. When he died, his humanity experienced death while his divine nature lived on, unable to die and went on to preach the gospel to the spirits in Sheol before being reunited with his resurrected body. However, there are not two Jesuses; as the Chalcedonian Creed affirms, he was fully God and fully man.

2. Both Ben and his wife, Jessica, have turned from hardened skepticism to genuine faith in Jesus. All of their doubts and struggles haven't evaporated, but they are anchored by the hope of Christ, living new lives for him. You can watch a short film about their journey from doubt to faith here: www.raisedbook.com.

CHAPTER 13: SEEKING APPROVAL

1. David Wells, *God in the Whirlwind: How the Holy-love of God Reorients Our World* (Wheaton, IL: Crossway, 2014), 34–35.

2. James D. G. Dunn, "Prayer," in *Dictionary of Jesus and the Gospels* (ed. Joel B. Green and Scot McKnight; Downers Grove, IL: InterVarsity Press, 1992), 619.

CHAPTER 14: EVANGELISM IN COMMUNITY

1. Richard V. Peace, "Conflicting Understandings of Christian Conversion: A Missiological Challenge," 8–14 (see n. 2 on p. 209).

2. This is why we have structured our church around missional communities—a structure of the church that gathers and sends groups of people on a common mission. This mission can be "home based," but is also embedded in the cultural fabric of the city. For instance, some city groups are focused on artists on the east side of the city, while others are intentionally making disciples downtown

through happy hours and hi-rise condo events. For more resources on missional communities, visit www.gcmcollective.org.

3. John P. Dickson, *Mission-Commitment in Ancient Judaism and in the Pauline Communities: The Shape, Extent and Background of Early Christian Mission* (Wissenschaftliche Untersuchungen zum Alten und Neuen Testament 2/159; Tübingen: Mohr Siebeck, 2003). In a review of Dickson's monograph, Kent Yinger notes: "He discounts popular proof-texts traditionally taken to reflect an expectation that Paul's churches (= every believer) would actively engage in local and regional mission (so O'Brien; cf. 1 Thess. 1.8; Phil. 1.27; 2.15-16; Eph. 6.15, 17). This sets the stage for a two-dimensional view of mission (p. 177): apostolic heralds proclaimed, congregations partnered with them in a variety of ways (i.e., promoted mission)" (Kent L. Yinger, "Review of *Mission-Commitment in Ancient Judaism and in the Pauline Communities,*" *Journal for the Study of the New Testament* 27 no. 1 [2004]: 117). This distinction should not diminish our value of evangelism, but rather expand our commitment to communally shaped practices that contribute to the promotion of the gospel. Dickson expands on this thesis in the popular level book, *The Best Kept Secret of Christian Mission: Promoting the Gospel with More Than Our Lips* (Grand Rapids: Zondervan, 2010).

4. For a full explanation of this idea see my *Gospel-Centered Discipleship*, 105–17.

5. Joseph H. Hellerman, *When the Church Was a Family: Recapturing Jesus' Vision for Authentic Christian Community* (Nashville: Broadman & Holman, 2011), 123–24.

6. Steve Timmis, *Everyday Church: Gospel Communities on Mission* (Wheaton, IL: Crossway, 2013), 111.

7. Green, *Evangelism in the Early Church*, 318.

CONCLUSION: SPIRIT-LED WITNESS

1. For a helpful treatment of how our evangelism, prayer, and the sovereignty of God work together, see J. I. Packer, *Evangelism and the Sovereignty of God* (Downers Grove, IL: InterVarsity Press, 2001).

INDEX

double-mindedness, 106

Edwards, Jonathan, 88
Eightfold Noble Path, 73, 77
euangelion, 119
evangelism. *See also* gospel
apologetics and, 45, 87–94, 98, 215n4
believable evangelism, 14–15
clarity for, 105–22
communal evangelism, 194–96
in community, 191–99
defeaters of, 12, 14, 30
definition of, 26–29, 56
diversity and, 123–32
explanation of, 26–29, 56
fluency in gospel, 133–39, 219n4
friendships and, 35–38
good evangelism, 47–48, 63, 127
message of, 29–30, 205–6
methods of, 29–30
misunderstanding, 11–12
"modern" forms of, 11–12
motivation of, 29–30
personal evangelism, 194–96
pressure of, 19–24, 202
as "project," 36–40, 48–51
proselytizing and, 53–63
recovering from, 11–12
re-evangelization, 100–103, 105–15
relationships and, 35–38
reshaping, 57–58
slow evangelism, 48–49
understanding, 29–30
as war, 204–5
Evangelism Explosion, 22, 210n7
Evangelism in the Early Church, 88
Every Good Endeavor, 43

failure, handling, 18–19
faith
in God, 42, 45, 48, 58, 96
in Jesus, 13, 23–28, 39–43, 55–60, 80, 86, 108, 129–31, 137–38, 149, 157
relationships and, 35–38

sharing, 19–24
workplace and, 37–43
false gods, 40, 56, 174
Five Pillars of Islam, 73–74, 77
fluency, speaking with, 133–39, 219n4
Four Spiritual Laws, 22–23, 43, 211n9
Frame, John, 91
friendships, 35–38. *See also* relationships
Frost, Michael, 48

Gamaliel, Rabbi, 88
God
faith in, 42, 45, 48, 58, 96
gospel of, 63
law of, 70, 177
nature of, 73–74, 91
power of, 201–2, 207
tolerance of, 69–70
gospel. *See also* evangelism
of adoption, 108–9, 154, 185, 188–89, 218n7
believable gospel, 12–15, 55, 97–98, 126–27, 138–42, 157–58, 164–65, 189, 205–6
communicating, 205–6, 217n1
complexity of, 110–11
cosmic gospel, 111–12, 117–21, 143
cultural engagement for, 133–36
cultural key for, 133–36
definition of, 111
dimensions of, 109–22
in everyday life, 13, 205–6
explanation of, 110–11
of God, 63
as good news, 12–13, 22–23, 111–13, 117–21, 205–6
historical gospel, 111–14
of Jesus, 18, 74, 77, 126–27, 178
of kingdom, 121, 216n4
message of, 29–30, 205–6
metaphors of, 14, 29–30, 122, 127–32, 147–58, 162–69, 205–7
misunderstanding, 11–12

There Will Be Blood, 11
Timmis, Steve, 198
tolerance
 classical tolerance, 68–70, 83
 of God, 69–70
 humility and, 74–79
 new tolerance, 71–72, 83
 persuasive tolerance, 80–83
 redemptive tolerance, 178–80
 of religious pluralism, 72–83
 seeking, 173–80
 understanding, 67–68
Tolkien, J. R. R., 120
Turkle, Sherry, 35
Two Ways to Live, 43, 211n9

unbelievable gospel, 17–18, 22–24.
 See also gospel

uninformed witness, 85–98. *See also*
 witness
"union with Christ" metaphor,
 128–31, 162–64, 167–69

White Noise, 105
witness
 impersonal witness, 30–52
 intolerant witness, 65–83
 preachy witness, 53–63
 Spirit-led witness, 201–7
 uninformed witness, 85–93
worldview Christianity, 34, 83, 92,
 175, 215n6

Zacharias, Ravi, 91